DATE DUE

30 505 JOSTEN'S

THE HARDEST LESSON

THE HARDEST LESSON

Personal Accounts
of a School Desegregation Crisis

by Pamela Bullard and Judith Stoia

Little, Brown and Company

BOSTON   TORONTO

COPYRIGHT © 1980 BY PAMELA BULLARD AND JUDITH STOIA

FIRST EDITION

Library of Congress Cataloging in Publication Data

Bullard, Pamela.
  The hardest lesson.

  SUMMARY: Describes how the desegregation of the
Boston schools in the 1970's affected the lives of
selected individual students and several adults,
chosen to represent a cross section of the community.
  1. School integration—Massachusetts—Boston—
Juvenile literature. [1. School integration—
Massachusetts—Boston] I. Stoia, Judith, joint
author. II. Title.
LC214.23.B67B84   370.19'342   79-23895
ISBN 0-316-11477-4

BP

*Published simultaneously in Canada
by Little, Brown & Company (Canada) Limited*

PRINTED IN THE UNITED STATES OF AMERICA

To Juli and Nick,

who deserve a world without hate

Acknowledgments

For being the first to believe in this book, thank you to John Langone.

For their valuable comments and criticism, we would like to thank Anne Heller and Ed Baumeister. For her initial support and enthusiasm, a special thanks to Ellen Jackson.

To Ann Steinetz, whose understanding of the delicacy of young life added a unique dimension to the manuscript, thank you.

And to Muriel Cohen, who many years ago so honestly began sharing her insight, knowledge, and concern about the city and its schools, we are especially grateful.

And to all the children, parents, teachers, and administrators who over the years have so generously shared their experiences with us . . . thank you.

Contents

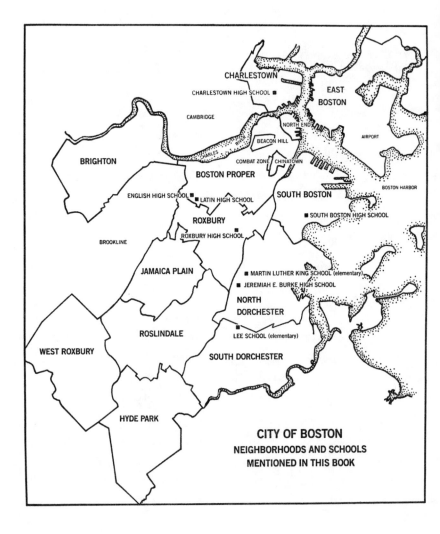

CITY OF BOSTON
NEIGHBORHOODS AND SCHOOLS
MENTIONED IN THIS BOOK

THE
HARDEST
LESSON

Introduction

HIS BLOND HAIR was matted, his gray T-shirt soiled. He was about twelve years old and he zigged and zagged his way clumsily to the front of the sidewalk crowd. He seemed solemn, at first, as he looked at the yellow school bus sitting fifteen yards in front of him. He smiled nervously at the people around him, then glanced over his shoulder. When he looked back toward the bus, he was angry. He squinted his eyes, pursed his mouth, clenched his teeth.

And then we saw it. The brick. He didn't try to hide it. Quickly, he raised his arm and, with a shriek, pegged the brick through a bus window. He appeared to be thrilled at the sounds of smashing glass and the cries of young children.

The blond boy was a hero. Parents and grandparents cheered him, slapped him on the back. Others picked up their own rocks, bottles, and bricks. In moments, the bus was under siege from all sides as it stood trapped at a red light.

Inside the bus, black children huddled under the seats, trying to protect themselves from the shattering glass and hail of rocks. They screamed as they stared at the rocks and bottles lying on the floor next to them.

A child stared at the brick. The brick had, in a few seconds, transformed Boston from the cradle of liberty to a national symbol of racial hatred.

We were, by chance, riding in a car behind that bus when the first brick was thrown. It was the first day of school, 1974, and buses carrying black junior-high students were leaving South Boston, the bastion of the anti-busing movement. Although there had been angry crowds shouting, "Nigger go home!" in the streets that morning, the day had been nonviolent. As the buses left the community, everyone was breathing a sigh of relief.

But then the brick was thrown and the battle joined. We did not know then that we were watching the first assault in a battle that would rage for years. A battle that not only pitched black against white, but father against son, friend against friend. It set neighborhoods against politicians, kids against cops, teachers against parents.

Desegregation touched everything and everyone in Boston. Whether you were a single mother living in a housing project or a young professional couple weighing the merits of settling in the city, desegregation changed your life in some way. The city would never be the same. Most importantly — and sometimes most tragically — the children who went through desegregation would never be the same.

This book is their story, their lesson in desegregation,

their experience in how human beings treat each other. Their stories may have meaning for many, but they are unique to the individuals involved. Their stories were told against the backdrop of a special, troubled city and a peculiar string of events that led to court-ordered desegregation.

Boston is usually described as one of America's most livable cities — a sophisticated, busy, urban core ringed by charming ethnic neighborhoods. About 20 percent of its population is black. A quick tour:

DOWNTOWN BOSTON is one of the busiest sections of the city, with its restaurants, department stores, theaters, and financial district. It holds much of Boston's history, too, on the gracious residential streets of Beacon Hill and the Back Bay, where the old-line Bostonians and newer, wealthier residents live. The downtown area, which also boasts the Boston Common, Public Garden and golden-domed State House, is a main attraction for the thousands of tourists who visit the city each year.

CHINATOWN sits on the edge of the theater district. It is the unhappy neighbor of an adult-entertainment district, with X-rated movies and pornography shops, and it struggles to maintain its sense of unity. Not nearly as large as the Chinese communities in some other large cities, Boston's Chinatown remains a close-knit neighborhood where many residents still speak their native language.

THE NORTH END also maintains strong bonds with the

home country. Italians settled the North End generations ago and still faithfully observe the traditional religious holidays. Many residents, some of whom speak Italian as their first language, sell fresh vegetables from pushcarts on the weekends. The North End, home of Paul Revere and the Old North Church, is overwhelmingly white, but not as resistant to black schoolchildren as some other white neighborhoods.

Ironically, the three neighborhoods with the most in common, South Boston, Charlestown, and Roxbury, were the three that hated each other the most during the early days of desegregation. The three have the lowest incomes in the city, the lowest levels of education (fewer than 35 percent of the residents finish high school) and the highest unemployment. But there is one striking difference: South Boston and Charlestown are virtually all white and especially resistant to blacks, and Roxbury is virtually all black (though not nearly as resistant to whites).

SOUTH BOSTON is fiercely Irish and boasts of its intolerance of outsiders, especially blacks. Southie, as it is known, is a working-class neighborhood that is perhaps more closely knit than any other part of Boston. Many people are born in South Boston, attend school there, find jobs, marry, and raise their own families in Southie. It's the only neighborhood with its own song: "Southie Is My Home Town." The arrival of forced desegregation threatened to ruin much of this community spirit and helped make South Boston a stiff center of resistance.

CHARLESTOWN is very much the cousin of South Boston.

Also the home of working-class Irish, Charlestown suffers from the same high unemployment, low educational levels, and low incomes as Southie. There is a long-standing, friendly rivalry between the two on the football field and on the basketball court. Perhaps because of this, Charlestown was determined to go Southie one better when, in the second year of desegregation, forced busing finally reached Charlestown.

Roxbury may be like Charlestown and South Boston when it comes to statistics on unemployment and income, but there the comparison stops. Roxbury is almost totally black, although many white people work in Roxbury or travel through the community on their way downtown. (Blacks could not work in or travel through South Boston or Charlestown.) A sprawling section of the city, Roxbury includes burned-out projects on its southern side and perfectly groomed old homes on the north. It is a complex community with varying populations and varying attitudes. It is, on the whole, the city's poorest neighborhood. Most of the black students bused into white neighborhoods came from Roxbury.

West Roxbury is like Roxbury only in name. West Roxbury is Boston's most affluent neighborhood; people here earn twice as much as people in Roxbury. It looks like any suburb in America — tree-shaded streets, two-car garages, a populace overwhelmingly white middle class. West Roxbury families could afford to send their children to private schools instead of to the black neighborhoods, where many were assigned. Some, though, took a chance and stayed in the public schools, and were often pleased that they did.

JAMAICA PLAIN is as diverse as any neighborhood in the city; a large Spanish population in one corner, proud, older Irish families in the other. Large stately homes combine with simple three-family apartments and desolate housing projects. It is one of the most peaceful, integrated communities in Boston.

HYDE PARK rides the southern flank of the city. Predominantly white middle- and working-class families are still nervous about the occasional black family that moves in. Hyde Park High was the scene of sporadic racial violence both before and after court-ordered desegregation.

DORCHESTER is an important seat of Irish power in Boston. The Irish settled there when they first arrived in Boston a century ago. In those days, it was the Irish who were the victims of blatant discrimination. (Shops often posted the sign, HELP WANTED, IRISH NEED NOT APPLY). By sheer numbers and organization, the Irish finally took over most elective offices in the city until today nearly every important city office is held by a person of Irish descent. As the Irish could afford to move "up" into neighborhoods previously closed to them, black families began moving into Dorchester. Bostonians now commonly refer to "North Dorchester," where black families live, and "Dorchester," still inhabited by the Irish. Despite the ethnic differences, racial conflicts are few.

* * *

Even a casual drive through Boston today shows that most neighborhoods are segregated. Some are because they developed that way; others, especially South Boston and Charlestown, because they were determined to keep it that way.

Those communities didn't want blacks in their neighborhoods, and they didn't want blacks in their schools. To that end, they elected people to the Boston School Committee who promised to keep their schools all white. Even though South Boston and Charlestown and parts of Dorchester were not the biggest section of the city, people there turned out in heavy numbers to vote for school-board members who were friendly to their point of view.

The most notorious politician to ride the anti-black issue was Louise Day Hicks, first a school-committee woman, later a city councillor. There would be no blacks in Southie and no white children bused out as long as Louise Day Hicks was in office. Her rallying cry was, "Never!"

For years, the Boston School Committee intentionally kept the public schools segregated while the city fathers looked the other way. In the process of separating white from black, the city, without apology, forgot about the black students. They attended school in the shabbiest buildings, were taught by the least experienced teachers and used the most archaic supplies, if there were supplies at all. Of the five thousand teachers in the city, only four hundred were black. Most of them taught in the inferior black schools.

In 1972, a group of black parents filed suit against the city of Boston and the school department, accusing them of willfully segregating the public schools, violating the constitutional rights of black students. Two years later, after a massive investigation, Federal Judge W. Arthur Garrity, Jr., agreed. On June 21, he ordered the city to desegregate its schools immediately.

Nothing happened.

Instead, politicians assured their constituents that children would never be bused in Boston, despite the judge's order. They organized rallies and parades, motorcades and speeches. They persuaded many white people, especially in South Boston and Charlestown, that if they just protested loudly enough, desegregation would go away.

Black parents were eager for a plan to desegregate the schools, insisting they had been robbed of an equal education long enough. In the middle of the hostilities were thousands of children and parents, black and white, who just wanted to get on with it and get it over with.

Nonetheless, city leaders, school officials and angry parents spent that first summer before desegregation stalling. The court finally approved a makeshift plan to bus white students to black neighborhoods and black students to white neighborhoods. But it was a rush job. The parents who weren't opposed to desegregation were still confused. What would their children's new school be like? Would the buses be safe? No one knew the answers. All they knew was that Boston was ill prepared for its day in history.

The first indication of how deeply the anti-busing passions ran came a few days before school opened. A rally on city hall plaza drew ten thousand angry anti-busers. Senator Edward Kennedy, Boston's favorite son, came to speak. But Kennedy was not there to endorse the anti-busing sentiment. The crowd knew he and his brothers had fought hard down the civil rights road, and they would not tolerate him.

In an ugly confrontation, Kennedy was forced to make a run for his office. A group of protestors broke off, pursued him, pummeled him with eggs and rocks, and finally smashed a plate-glass window in Kennedy's office building.

That evening, large signs were posted around the city with just four letters on them: ROAR. It stood for "Restore Our Alienated Rights," and was to become the theme of an anti-busing organization set up by Louise Day Hicks. It would grow into the nation's largest anti-busing force, with branches in several American cities.

As the buses of black children climbed the hill to South Boston High School that first day of school, ROAR placards greeted them. The blacks next saw screaming whites. Then the police.

Throughout that first day, Boston waited anxiously. Perhaps the city would make it through without incident. After all, in most neighborhoods, black and white, residents paid no attention to the buses. But as the buses were leaving Southie at the end of the school day, the brick was thrown and the battle was on.

Southie glowed in triumph. An otherwise peaceful first day of desegregation had been ruined. The television networks that night led with the story of racial hatred on the streets of Boston. Despite the fact that the vast majority of Boston's schools desegregated peacefully, even happily in some cases, the city's image was now one of violence and fear.

Violence was sporadic that first year. One day would be calm, the next day an incident involving two students jostling in a cafeteria line would snowball into a riot. Throughout the city, racial incidents in the schools would trigger racial incidents in the neighborhoods. In Southie, a black man was dragged from his car and beaten. In Roxbury, black kids from the housing project lay in wait for white passersby, their artillery of bricks and bottles at hand.

And even though the violence was not widespread, when it did surface, it was very real, very frightening. On two occasions, the city was on the brink of having federal troops come in to keep the peace. Once, President Gerald Ford put the 101st Airborne Division on "increased readiness" for duty on the streets of this historic American city.

Through it all, a pattern developed that was to continue for much of Boston's desegregation experience. The anti-busing leaders of ROAR were courted by politicians and pursued by the press. An unemployed sheet-metal worker in South Boston would imperiously call press conferences to respond to the day's events and the press would all attend. The parents, black and white, who went along quietly with desegregation — and they were, after all, the vast majority — were ignored. Neither the press nor the politicians flocked to their side, much less to their cause. Their quiet compliance didn't make good head-lines, and their lack of organization didn't deliver enough votes.

The city limped through the 1974 school year with the worried realization that more was yet to come. The schools were only partially desegregated in 1974. The next school year would see even more busing, for the first time involving neighborhoods that were potentially as explo-sive as Southie had been. That summer the city collec-tively bit its nails.

The second year of desegregation saw Southie targeted for trouble again, as was Charlestown, which was being desegregated for the first time. This time, the authorities were ready. City and police officials were determined not to be embarrassed again by their lack of preparation.

Opening day 1975 saw a massive police presence in South Boston and Charlestown. There were 1,000 Boston Police, three hundred fifty State Police, two hundred fifty Metropolitan District Commission Police, federal mar-shals, and, waiting nearby, six hundred National Guards-men.

The reporters, as usual, stood in a no-man's-land between the police and the crowd. We stamped our feet in the cold autumn air and looked around: hundreds of police in full riot gear, a ragtag band of kids from the Charlestown housing project. We put our money on the kids.

Off and on that fall, the kids led police on wild chases through the twisting corridors of the projects in Charlestown and South Boston. There was hit-and-run violence in the streets and in some schools. In April, a black man was attacked with the staff of an American flag by a group of white students on City Hall Plaza. A picture of the attack blazed on front pages around the world. In another act of violence a white man was dragged from his car and viciously beaten by black youths. He lapsed into a coma, never regaining consciousness. He died two years later.

In a move of desperation, Boston's Mayor Kevin White, who, throughout, had walked a tight wire between the pro- and anti-desegregation forces, called for a Procession Against Violence through the streets of Boston. Fifty thousand, who had remained quiet for so long, rushed to show their faith in the city and their yearning for peaceful desegregation. They were led by U.S. senators, the governor, U.S. representatives, city officials. Black and white, middle class and working class, they marched. Conspicuously absent were the anti-busers, who branded the march for peace a "farce."

Slowly over the summer and into the third year of forced desegregation, the hard edge of racial hatred began to dull. Some people grew weary of the unending and unfruitful protests. Others finally realized that the politicians they had followed so faithfully into battle were powerless to stop a federal court order, no matter what the demagogues had promised. Some parents left the city, some sent their children to private schools, many reluctantly returned to the public school system, often surprised at the new coats of paint, updated supplies and modern programs that came as a result of the court's involvement.

Yet the toll on Boston was severe. White students left the public schools in droves. Racial hostility thrived where it had never surfaced before. Mobility in the city for both blacks and whites, but much more so for blacks, was drastically reduced. Today there are still a few neighborhoods in Boston where a black person simply cannot go.

The costs were staggering: $13 million in police costs alone in 1975. And Boston now had a national reputation as a city of hate.

Still, many of the injustices had been corrected. Blacks were no longer sentenced to inferior schools. In a school system long regarded as substandard, education was upgraded for everyone, black and white. Black teachers were hired. Prestigious universities, that had always shared the resources of the city but few of its problems, were paired with public schools to enrich the educational atmosphere. Local businesses also helped out.

Did desegregation have any immediate benefits? After the second year of desegregation, black students registered a slight gain in reading skills; previously they had ranked far below the national average. White students suffered no loss in reading levels.

But one of the biggest changes brought by desegregation was among the least expected: for the first time, parents became intensely involved in the schools. At first it was a question of safety for their children. But then they discovered that a teacher wasn't giving homework or their child didn't know how to multiply. They became active in every facet of education.

Today, most schools and neighborhoods are quiet. Raging crowds no longer greet the buses. Police seldom escort them in and out of neighborhoods or patrol the hallways. Anti-busing demonstrations are a thing of the past. Anti-busing politicians, including Mrs. Hicks, have lost much of their clout. Even South Boston High School is free of the police officers who once filled the halls and guarded the streets.

Despite a stretch of calm in the city, there are grim reminders that racism is still a part of the city's fabric. In September 1979, masked white youths stoned buses carrying black children through South Boston. A few weeks later, a black football player was shot by a sniper as he stood in the end zone of the Charlestown football field. As of this writing, he is paralyzed from the neck down. But unlike such events in the past, this incident in 1979 horrified the entire city, including the Charlestown community.

Federal Judge W. Arthur Garrity is still deeply involved. He says he is still not convinced that the Boston School Committee and the city can be trusted to provide an equal education for all children. He is still watching over the city's shoulder, trying to make sure that any gains made in desegregation will not be eroded away.

The school system itself has changed substantially. It is no longer run entirely by political patronage. Many of the schools and programs can rival those in the affluent suburbs. The court order was, unquestionably, the catalyst for change in the city's schools. Change that was desperately needed for a school system that ignored black students and failed to provide adequate education for large numbers of white students.

But what of the students themselves, who have been at the center of this long and bitter struggle? How much do they feel has been gained through desegregation? For them, has the prize been worth the battle? For some, it has been worth it. For some, it has not. But each one of them has experienced a piece of American history — good and bad.

We wrote this book because we believed their stories should be told. We've heard from the psychologists, the politicians, the educators. But the students who daily lived through desegregation have been silent. And it is perhaps their simple stories that are the most important lessons of all.

This book is a collection of the stories of individual students, as well as three adults whose lives were touched by students going through desegregation. The people were selected from hundreds of interviews over the years. We have sat in their living rooms, met their families, often sat in their classrooms. Their conversations have been recorded, the stories they told investigated and authenticated.

All were eager to be interviewed, but some demanded that their names be changed. Since in some communities compliance with desegregation is still tantamount to an act of betrayal, and since some students were only willing to tell their stories if their parents were not told, we complied with that request.

In some cases, it was necessary to change a street name, or even the name of a specific school, if it was not fundamental to the story, to protect a student's identity.

One person's name, however, is unchanged — Charlie Ray, headmaster of Roxbury High. Over the years, he has become a friend and a source of inspiration. His school is unique, as he is, and there is no way to disguise him.

Charlie Ray believes in his kids — all kids — black, white, Asian, Indian, Spanish. He believes in their future, and so do we. That's why we want to tell their story.

Boston
October 1979

Julie

A FEW DAYS before school opened, Julie decided on a daring expedition. Not to faraway places, but only a few miles from her home. She was going to visit South Boston.

For a black sophomore from Roxbury, Boston's black community, it was a bold decision. South Boston had made it clear for a long time that it didn't welcome blacks, even as visitors. The year before, black students had been bused to Southie for the first time. South Boston residents had reacted with angry, violent demonstrations. This year they promised more of the same.

Still, Julie was curious about this community where she would be attending school in a couple of days, and she wanted to take a look at it. She knew it was a working-class Irish neighborhood, but she didn't know much more. She thought it was odd that even though she had grown up in Boston, there was one neighborhood she had never seen.

Julie was determined to be cool about her trip. She was going to act as if she knew exactly what she was doing. She was not going to act scared. That was on the outside.

Inside, Julie was shaking, and she knew it. It wasn't just that she was disobeying her parents, because in a way she wasn't. They had never actually told her not to go to South Boston. Why would any black want to go to Southie? That's why Julie's stomach felt like bubbling oatmeal. She told herself she just wanted to take a quick look.

It was a peaceful Sunday afternoon on Labor Day weekend when the subway rolled into Andrew station. Julie's heart picked up its pace. "This is the place," she thought, "Southie. Looks quiet, clean, no trouble."

The subway doors snapped closed behind her and Julie began walking towards the exit sign. White people passed her without so much as a second look, and she started to feel a little braver.

Out in the bright sunlight, she noticed how neat and orderly these Southie streets were. An elderly lady ambled past her and smiled. Julie shyly smiled back and began strolling down the street next to the station feeling a little more confident. She even wondered why everyone worried about going to school in this quiet, sleepy neighborhood. There seemed to be very few people about, only a man walking toward her. He seemed hardly to notice as she brushed by. But suddenly she felt a wetness, a stickiness on her face. At first, she didn't know what it was and stood there perplexed, wiping the slimy stuff off. Then, as she looked at her hand, she realized someone had just spat at her and hit her right in the face. She swung around to see the man she had just passed. He half-turned, half-smiled, then walked on, whistling.

Julie was confused. The man seemed about her father's age, neatly dressed with an athletic letter jacket that said "Southie" on it. His face didn't look mean or hateful. And she hadn't done anything to bother him. She wiped the rest of the spit off and turned back toward the subway station. The neighborhood still seemed sleepy and safe — she wondered if the spitting incident had really happened.

No one seemed to be about. "Maybe they're all still having Sunday dinner," Julie thought as she crossed the street and fumbled in her pocket for change for the subway.

Suddenly she wondered why she hadn't noticed the group of boys sooner. They were lounging on the corner near a luncheonette.

"You lost, nigger? Can't you find the zoo? Want a banana?"

Julie quickened her pace. She was glad she had not gone too far. She slammed a quarter in the turnstyle and raced down the steps, thanking God she heard a train coming. A glance back told her the boys had jumped over the turnstyles and were following her. She ran onto the train as the boys, walking slowly now, made monkey gestures from the platform and sang, "Bye, bye, blackbird."

The train pulled away, but Julie could still see the boys

taunting her. As she sat down, she realized that the people on the car, all of them white, were staring at her. Julie turned and looked out the window, trying to get lost in the blackness of the subway tunnel, hoping they wouldn't notice her tears, her hands shaking in her lap.

The first day of school arrived bright and warm, but Julie shivered as she looked through the faded curtains at the morning she dreaded.

She pulled the sheet up over her head and remembered past years when she had looked forward to school. Not this year. Especially not after what had happened Sunday.

"Julie, move!" shouted her mother from downstairs.

She crawled out of bed and carefully put on her new skirt and the blouse her mother had stayed up late to iron the night before. Pulling the comb through her hair, she watched her face carefully in the mirror, surprised she looked so calm.

When Julie walked into the kitchen, she knew right away something was wrong. Her mother was usually bustling around, singing along with the radio. This morning, though, she was working grimly at the stove and there was no music at all.

"This stupid South Boston business," her mother said angrily. "The radio's full of news of the police over there this morning. . . . If we didn't want you to finish your high school education, we'd yank you right out of there."

"It's gonna be OK," Julie tried to reassure her mother, knowing herself that it would be far from OK. "Maybe after all the fightin' there last year, those white kids will leave us alone."

"You just remember, Julie, live and let live. If they don't bother with you, you don't bother with them."

Julie knew it wasn't going to be that easy. When she met her girlfriend Lynn outside to walk to the bus stop, she admitted she was scared.

"Just cool it, gotta play it cool. That's what my brother says," Lynn said.

"Yeah, he oughta know. That brother of yours."

"Say what?"

"Thinkin' of him goin' to Southie last year gives me the shakes."

"How come?"

"He was suspended what? Twelve times for fightin'? Came home with a broken nose once? You think talkin' about him makes me feel better?"

"I hear ya."

About ten other kids were waiting on the corner for the bus. The ones who had been to South Boston High the year before were kidding, but only half-kidding, about how bad it was.

"It was so bad," one boy joked, "they didn't ask you to erase the blackboard, they asked you to erase the whiteboard!"

While everyone laughed, Julie stared at the empty beer bottles and crumpled cigarette packs lying in the gutter at her feet. This morning, even the grimy streets of Roxbury offered some sense of security.

"You carrying any protection, sister?" asked one boy.
"What do you mean?"

"You know, a knife or pick or something." He showed
her a pocketknife stuck in the lining of his jacket. "You're
crazy if you don't. Wait till they corner you in the hallway between classes and you all alone. This can be your
best friend." He patted his pocket.

Julie's stomach began to hurt. She didn't want to fight,
and she didn't want to get into trouble. Right now she
just wanted to go home.

Julie and Lynn grabbed seats in the front of the bus,
since Julie was still determined to have a good look at the
place where she was going to have to go to school. Her
brief visit Sunday hadn't told her much about Southie
itself, although it had told her something about some of
the people.

Slowly, the dirty, dull streets of Roxbury changed to
cleaner, neater streets as the bus approached South Boston.
Julie thought that even the houses seemed brighter —
yellows, greens, reds — not like the monotone of her
neighborhood. They passed through the integrated community of Dorchester, and as more black students piled
on and more jokes were told, everyone started sounding
braver and braver.

Finally the bus began to travel the half-mile stretch
along the beaches into the heart of Southie. Everyone
suddenly was silent, except for one lone voice from the
back that said resignedly, "Here we go. . . ."

As the bus swung onto the main boulevard, four police

motorcycles pulled in front, their blue lights flashing. Julie looked in back of the bus and saw four more motorcycle policemen. She didn't know if all the police made her feel better or worse.

She peered out the window anxiously and noticed the same neat rows of houses she had seen by the subway station. But, to her surprise, there were no angry crowds gathered along the bus route. Maybe the radio had been wrong. Julie breathed a sigh of relief and watched the sun dance on the waters off Carson Beach. It was all so quiet.

"Hey, look over there," someone yelled. Everyone turned to see a greeting scrawled in big red letters along a fence by the road: "Niggers Go Home." Then on the sidewalk a few blocks up: "Resist!"

Just at that moment, the bus turned a corner and began its slow climb up a steep hill. The motorcycle police in front signaled the bus to stop. As the police talked on their walkie-talkies, Julie and her classmates waited in silence. The bus sat in the middle of an empty street. On either side squatted small, trim houses that crowded right up against the street, making it seem even closer inside the yellow school bus. Julie and Lynn stared at the "Nigger Go Home" signs written on paper taped to the windows of the houses. It seemed like every house carried a message: "No Forced Busing," "Never," "KKK," "White Power."

Julie looked up the hill in front to see what was causing the delay. Through the blue flashing lights of the police, she could see the gray, foreboding bulk of South

Boston High School looming like an old fort from the top of the hill. It looked even more unfriendly in person than it did in television news stories.

Finally the bus began inching up the hill. Everyone inside seemed to hold his breath. As they crept closer to the school, Julie saw why they had waited down below.

A large crowd of angry people milled in front of the high school. The mob, which covered several blocks, was screaming, shoving, and throwing rocks and bottles at the police, who were trying to push it back.

Julie had never seen police dressed like this before. They were like paratroopers in the war movies, wearing one-piece suits and high military boots, with their helmets pulled down to cover their faces. Guns swung from their hips, and they gripped long, shiny, black sticks in their hands. Some of them had gas masks hanging from their necks.

These police were joined by others on horses. Still more police strained to control attack dogs that tugged at their thick leather leashes. Julie could see column after column of helmeted police marching from behind the school and from the side streets to add to the chaos.

"Oh, Jesus," someone in the back of Julie said. "I wish to God I never got on this bus."

"Just stay cool, stay cool," said a local minister who was riding the bus with them. "The police will keep them away from you." But push as they might, the police could only cut a thin path for the bus to creep through.

Julie remembered the young boys from Sunday and

wondered if they were in this crowd. Or the man who spat at her. As the screams grew louder, Julie matched faces with voices. They were all ages, little children as well as grandparents. Hundreds of angry whites raised their clenched fists and screeched at the buses.

"Go home, nigger!"

"Out of Southie!"

Julie was shocked to see three women her mother's age dressed up in bandanas with little ribbons all through their hair, their faces painted black. They were waving watermelons at the buses. She had never seen grown women act like that; her own mother always seemed so dignified to her. Her dismay gave way to anger. She realized the women were pleased at the frightened black faces they saw in the school bus windows. Their pleasure made her furious.

Finally the bus pulled up to the thick wrought-iron fence surrounding the school. A black man stepped onto the bus.

"OK, kids, now move off the bus, no shovin', up the front steps, don't turn around, don't say anything to anybody, don't even make a face."

When Julie stepped onto the sidewalk, the noise of the crowd grew even louder. Police and angry whites seemed to press in on her from everywhere. A confusing maze of cameras and microphones suddenly materialized around her. The police pushed the reporters back, but as Julie headed for the school a reporter shouted, "Are you scared?"

Julie clutched her notebook and bit her lip, trying to shut out the scene around her. She muttered under her breath, "You're damn right I'm scared, man, and you would be too if you was black."

Inside the door of Southie High, Julie relaxed a bit. "This is better," she told Lynn. "They can't get us here."

"Oh, yeah? Look."

Painted on the wall in front of them was, "Kill the niggers!" in bright red letters. A janitor was popping open cans of green paint to cover the slogan. Julie wondered why it hadn't been painted over before the black students arrived.

They were ordered into a single line and told to open all their pocketbooks and book bags. These would be searched for weapons. Then everyone had to pass through a metal detector.

Lynn looked at Julie and grimaced.

Julie shrugged. "Ever since that kid got stabbed last year, everybody's gotta do it." Still, there were stories that anyone who really wanted to smuggle anything into Southie could.

Waiting in line, Julie took a good look around her. Southie was an old school. The green paint curled and peeled from the walls everywhere. The dull brown floor tiles smelled as if they had recently been scrubbed, but no amount of cleaning could undo the generations of scarring and shuffling that left them torn and dented. The walls seemed close, unfriendly. Julie shivered.

Walking down the hall, Julie was startled to see more policemen in the corridors, still in their riot gear. They looked strange standing in a high school corridor, sipping coffee, billy clubs and handcuffs dangling from their belts. The corridors were quiet and dark. The two girls passed no white students.

"Maybe the white kids ain't comin' today," whispered Lynn hopefully.

As they opened the door to their homeroom, they heard an excited buzz of young voices. But as soon as they walked in, the room fell completely silent. The teacher motioned them in.

"Come in, girls, take a seat."

They looked around at a sea of white faces. Some were smirking. Some were angry. A few looked silently down at their desks. A single black boy sat in a corner, surrounded by empty desks.

"Gee, where do you think they can sit?" a white boy called out.

"Quiet!" the teacher ordered. "They may sit wherever they please."

"Yeah," another voice muttered, "As long as it's over there in Motown."

The white kids laughed loudly as Julie and Lynn made their way to seats next to the black boy. As they sat down, white students nearby pulled their desks farther away. The teacher had just started giving instructions when the bell rang and Julie was jolted into thinking about her first class. As the white students pressed toward the door, Julie and Lynn hesitated, watching the other black student.

"You better walk with me. I've been through this before. The hallway's the worst, and whatever you do, don't go to the bathrooms."

"Huh?"

"I mean it. They catch you in the bathroom and you're fair game. No teachers, no cops. Just an aide."

"An aide?" asked Julie.

"Yeah, you know, someone hired by the school to watch over us — along with all the cops. But you can't always count on 'em. Sometimes they're as bad as the kids."

They joined a group of black students in the hallway. Julie noticed that all the white students walked single file down one side of the hall, the black students down the other. Occasionally, the ranks were broken by a helmeted policeman who walked along, his eyes roving.

White and black students taunted each other relentlessly.

"Stick around after school, nigger, we'll teach you some real lessons."

"Get lost, honky, you couldn't pay me to stick around this hole."

Chemistry class was much the same as homeroom. Black students sat on one side of the room, white students on the other. Throughout the period, black and white students whispered insults and threats. Still, the teacher tried to ignore it all and conduct a routine first day. Near the end of the hour, the teacher broke off in midsentence and looked toward the door. He was listening.

The rumble began faintly, but soon everyone could hear it.

"Here we go, Southie! Here we go!"

People marching in the corridors were singing Southie's fight song. It was the same chanting the black students had heard outside. Now it was joined by shouts of, "Niggers eat shit!" and "Kill the niggers!"

"Jesus!" said a boy next to Julie. "They let those crazy people inside the school!"

The chanting grew louder. It sounded as if hundreds of people were marching in the halls, their voices booming off the walls, penetrating every classroom.

"Here we go, Southie! Here we go!"

"Ignore that, stay in your . . ."

The teacher's words were cut off by a white student's dashing for the door. He was joined by what seemed to be every white kid in the class. As he threw open the door, Julie could see the hall jammed with white students chanting and waving their fists in the air.

As the sounds of the demonstration grew fainter, the public address system crackled, "The remainder of today's classes are canceled. All white students must leave the building immediately. Buses will arrive in twenty minutes to take black students home."

"Oh, come on!" protested an impatient voice behind Julie. "I don't have time for this crap!"

Julie was surprised to see a white girl sitting there, slamming her books shut. In fact, there were four white students who had not joined the group.

The loud speaker came alive again. "Black students will file to the front door."

The teacher looked at the students. "It's all clear," he said as they walked past him. He tried to smile at Julie. "Be careful."

Once at the front door, Julie understood the warning. As she peered out the double front doors, she could see the long expanse of the school yard, enclosed by the black iron fence. Just beyond that, the waving fists and crude homemade signs of hundreds of white demonstrators promised a repeat of the morning's protest.

"What do they want now?" asked Lynn as she squeezed in next to Julie. "Here they're yellin' at us to go home and we're going just as fast as we can, and they're still yelling!"

"These people won't be happy 'til we're on a leaky boat back to Africa. Where are those buses, anyway?"

Julie felt scared all over again. The number of police looked tiny compared to the mob it was trying to hold back.

Julie remembered reading about a crowd of white people who had caught a school bus in the South. They rocked it back and forth with all the little kids inside and would have tipped it over if the police hadn't arrived at the last minute.

She saw a small caravan of buses moving up the hill as mounted police held back the crowd. The black students looked at each other nervously. Suddenly Roxbury seemed very far away, instead of just the couple of miles that it actually was. A policeman signaled toward the front of the school, and a teacher shouted, "OK, kids, let's go!"

The black students poured out of the doors and started to scramble down the stairs until someone yelled, "Don't run! Show 'em we ain't scared!"

With that, they slowed to a walk. Some even swaggered. Julie looked over at Lynn and noticed her smiling and even waving to the crowd and cameras. Julie herself smiled, going along with the show. The white crowd grew even more enraged. The shouts became angrier, and by the time Julie reached the bus, she was running.

As she collapsed into a seat, a policeman yelled, "Get this crate moving, before this crowd gets loose."

The buses began their slow descent. Police stood shoulder to shoulder on both sides of the street, a human barrier between the black students inside their buses and the white mob on the sidewalks.

As the buses rumbled down the hill, both blacks and whites shouted and made obscene gestures at each other.

The buses picked up speed as they neared the bottom of the hill. Through the flashing blue lights of the motorcycles surrounding the bus, Julie could see police in their paratrooper outfits guarding each intersection. As she looked out the back window at South Boston High, she picked out uniformed men standing on the roof with rifles. As the buses reached the bottom of the hill and made the long sweep along the beachfront, they passed by a large housing project. Julie's heart came to her throat. The sidewalks were packed with angry whites. This time, though, she knew there was not enough protection. The lines of police began to waver and break under the barrage of bricks and bottles hurled at each bus.

When it finally came, it sounded like an explosion.

"Watch out!" The window splintered and spread where the rock struck, spraying the two students in the seat with tiny slivers of glass. A boy grabbed his head and screamed, the splinters pricking and scratching his eyes. Blood trickled down his cheek and spilled onto his leather jacket.

"Oh, my God," the girl next to him gasped, her hands clutched in front of her. She was just reaching for him when the second rock crashed through three rows up. The bus filled with screams.

Julie's crouch was a reflex action. She heard the next rock strike the window a split second before it crashed through and smashed the cheek of a girl across the aisle. The girl's eyes widened in shock a moment before she screamed.

Suddenly, the bus was under siege from all sides. Beer bottles smashed through the front window. Two large rocks hit the middle aisle almost simultaneously. The mob surged and raged outside, now heaving bricks at each window. Julie hid her head in her hands, realizing that with every rock, they were getting closer and closer.

"Get under the seats! Get under the seats!"

Everyone dived for the floor as another rock came flying through a window. Julie crunched under a seat face down. The floor was wet and gummy and smelled bad. She felt dirty. She brushed her hand through her hair and felt slivers of glass prick her skin. Next to her, Lynn cried softly.

Suddenly they felt the bus jolt over what must have been a curb, then another. They could hear police outside yelling at the driver to floor it.

Gradually the shouts and sirens faded. Julie was sure they were out of Southie. Still no one moved. They stayed under the seats, feeling the bus sway with each turn.

"OK, everybody up!" called out the bus driver. "We made it."

The bus pulled to a halt and a policeman jumped on.

"Is anyone hurt badly?" He walked up and down the aisle, checking students. One girl was bleeding from her cheek. The boy who had glass splinters near his eye grabbed the policeman's hand. "Come with me in the cruiser." He helped them out of the bus, then turned to the driver.

"Get these kids home. It's been all over the radio, and their parents will be scared to death."

As the bus headed into Roxbury, Julie looked around. Five windows were shattered; their jagged edges made ugly patterns against the sky. Splinters of glass tinkled to the floor as students brushed off their hair and clothes.

The driver wound a handkerchief around his head and it quickly grew bright red. The window next to him was shattered.

"Why did they go after you? You're white."

"They don't care. They figure anyone who cooperates with this busing is a traitor."

The bus slowed and Julie was relieved to see they were back in her neighborhood. Dozens of anxious parents and neighbors, along with several camera crews and reporters, surrounded each bus as it pulled in.

The black students poured off the buses, some shouting angrily at reporters about what had happened, others still crying.

Julie and Lynn pushed through the crowd. Julie spotted her mother watching the students get off another bus. She was jumping up to try and find her daughter through the broken windows of the bus. She was crying.

"Momma, Momma, I'm OK."

"Julie, you all right, honey? Are you sure?" her mother sobbed as she opened her arms. "I heard all the news about the trouble and I couldn't think of nothin' to do. I wanted to go get you out, but I couldn't get near there."

"They hate us over there."

"I know, I see these buses."

"Momma, I don't want to go back. They can have their school all to themselves. It just ain't worth it."

"We don't have a choice, honey. No one said it was gonna be easy."

*   *   *

The next day, Julie kicked at the cigarette wrappers in the gutter and watched for the school bus. There were fewer black kids today. "That's no surprise," she thought.

The yellow bus turned the corner a block away and eased up against the curb next to them. Julie stood back, in no hurry. Finally, with a sigh, she stepped onto the bus and into her second day at South Boston High.

Greg and Laurie

GREG BOUNDED down the steps of the bus and tipped his cap to the side. He swaggered up to his English teacher, who was standing on the steps of South Boston High School, and laughed. "Hey, my main man! What's happening?"

"Gregory, where the hell have you been?" Matt Robinson extended his hand for the slap ritual. "It's Thursday. You haven't been to school all week."

"Hey. I was here Monday."

"Big deal. Listen, I've been looking for you. I want you to cool it at the school."

"I don't get you."

"This place is gonna blow any minute if things don't simmer down. So lay off the white kids, will you?"

"Good thing you're black, man, or I'd knock your damn head off."

Robinson tightened his grip on Greg's arm. "I mean this, Greg. You keep messin' with those kids, callin' them names and all and I personally am gonna kick your butt."

"How about them messin' with me?"

"We're talking to the white kids, too. But this thing is

so far out of control here that one little word could touch it off. You want to go to school or you want to fight all the time?"

"Hey, man, I been goin' here for four months, ever since school opened, and I haven't learned a damn thing yet."

"Because you spend all your time messin' with people."

"They're botherin' me, too," Greg insisted angrily, tearing his arm away. "You get them to lay off me."

He turned before Robinson could answer and ran up the steps two at a time into the high school. He walked through the lobby, past the half dozen police officers who watched students coming into the building.

"Hey, man, welcome back." Brian, another black student, slapped Greg on the back.

"Hey. What's happenin'?"

"Real shaky here lately. This place is gonna bust. Nobody talkin' to nobody. Fightin' all the time in the halls. Nobody pays attention to the teachers anymore. They can't do nothin'. Just call the cops."

"Hey, man, don't you like bein' in the vanguard?" They laughed. In this first year of busing, the black students attending South Boston high were often advised to think of themselves as pioneers, black explorers landing on foreign white soil. But day after day of hostile crowds on the streets and escalating tension inside the school had most of them swearing that if they didn't have to attend South Boston High School, they wouldn't.

Now, near the end of the first semester, the situation

was worse than ever. Instead of growing accustomed to each other, the white and black students daily moved farther apart. Just one bad incident, everyone said, would touch off a full-scale riot.

By now Greg, like other black students, was convinced he would never be tolerated by the white community. And he didn't have much tolerance for them. It was one of the many reasons fewer than half of the black students assigned to South Boston High School actually attended the first year. Some black parents were afraid and kept their kids at home to wait it out, even if it took a week, a month, or longer.

But Greg's family was like the majority. They resented the school years spent in run-down buildings with substandard materials and inexperienced staff. They felt that if the only way to get an education as good as the white community's was to bus their children there, then so be it.

Of course, families like Greg's also had little choice. They could not afford private school. If Greg was assigned to South Boston High School, that was where he had to go, like it or not.

"Hey, my favorite marshmallow!" Greg teased as he tipped his hat to a white girl standing with her friends by the front door. Greg's constant taunting made him especially unpopular with the white students.

"Watch it, bonehead, your bone head's showin'," responded Laurie with a sneer. The girls standing around her stopped chewing their gum long enough to laugh in agreement.

"You know, honky, one of these days I'm gonna put your mouth where your navel is. Now get outa my way." Greg felt himself growing angrier by the moment.

"What if I don't?" asked Laurie, feeling braver as her friends closed in around her, effectively blocking the doorway. "Maybe you're gonna have to go back to your slum."

With that, Greg lowered his shoulder and charged. He hit Laurie square in the shoulder and chest, knocking her hard to the ground. Laurie and her friends screamed around him as he turned to head down the hall. But the sound of people running told him it was too late.

"Hey, that's it, you two. Cut it out." A policeman hurried up the corridor as other students started to gather. Laurie was still screaming invectives at Greg.

"You two, upstairs to the holding rooms," the policeman said, referring to the rooms set aside at South Boston High School to hold students while they cooled off. Trouble in the school was so frequent, the rooms were often in use.

Matt Robinson came up behind Greg, grabbed his arm, and marched him upstairs.

"Good work, sucker. In the school thirty seconds and back in trouble. What did I just tell you? Why don't you just keep that mouth of yours shut?"

"Do you keep your mouth shut when you're bein' called nigger? Well, not me, man!"

"Then, at least at this school, you'll spend all your days in these holding rooms or on the streets."

Robinson closed the bottom section of the Dutch doors. Greg paced the small room for a minute, then walked to a wall and pounded it with his open hand, shouting a few angry examples of his street vocabulary.

Although Greg was a frequent tenant of the holding rooms, he never grew used to them. They were degrading, like little pens to keep animals in. Small, square, all concrete except for the wooden bench and the Dutch door open at the top.

Greg watched as Mr. Robinson walked to an identical holding room. It was used for white students.

"And you, Laurie," said Robinson to the white girl who leaned defiantly out the top of the door. "When are you and your friends gonna stop asking for trouble? This is a school we're trying to run. Didn't any teacher talk to you about taking it easy?"

"Yeah. Miss Munroe did." Laurie cracked her gum and stared directly at Robinson. "I told her it was a lot easier to be cool before the scum arrived." Robinson flinched but caught himself before he yelled at her.

"I'm getting real tired of your lip. I'm warning you to clean it up." Robinson stared coldly at her. "I'm going to see the headmaster and find out what we do with you two this time."

Laurie sat down nervously. She thought she might have pushed her luck too far this time. Robinson must really have been angry if he was checking with the headmaster. She had expected just to cool off down here, then be sent to her first class. But the trip to the headmaster meant disciplinary action. Last time, she wasn't allowed to attend cheerleading practice for a week, and that meant she was not allowed to cheer for Saturday's game.

Laurie thought being a cheerleader was one of the few things that was the way it used to be, before blacks came to Southie. Like most other white students, she had boycotted the first two weeks of school. Her parents couldn't afford parochial school (even if she could get in), and they worried about her going to school with blacks, whom they viewed as tough, street-smart kids from crime-infested neighborhoods.

But Laurie had no more choice about where she could go to school than Greg did. Besides, South Boston High School had always been for Southie, not for anyone else. So, after the boycott, Laurie and her friends returned to school, determined not to let the black students take it over. Back in school, hostilities had mounted, day after day, week after week.

"I hope you're pleased with yourself," she shouted out the door to Greg.

He didn't bother to answer. He was actually a little angry with himself because he kept getting involved in fights. It had been going on since September. Today, four months later, there was as much anger inside the school as there used to be on the streets. The white students still sat on one side of the classroom, the blacks on the other.

The newspapers and television stations reported that everything was calm inside Southie now. But Greg knew better. The place was a time bomb.

Greg heard Mr. Robinson walking down the hall, talking to another teacher.

"I know the faculty's exhausted, Jeanne, but what can we do? Go to the judge and say, 'Enough! This school just isn't going to work'?"

"Well, is it, Matt? They've created a monster here. Never should have tried to bus Roxbury and Southie the first year! It's bigger than us. It's bigger than the kids. They don't know how to handle it, and neither do we anymore."

"Hey. It's tough, but it's going to be worth it."

"I wonder. See you later."

"OK, you two. Headmaster's tied up. Get to your first class." Just then the bell rang, filling the corridor with students.

Some of Laurie's friends huddled around her, asking about her punishment. Smiling, Greg walked past the group and again tipped his hat. Laurie extended her middle finger in Greg's direction.

At that moment, a scream came from the other end of the corridor. Then more screams, and voices shouting. Greg ran toward the sounds, Laurie and her friends close behind. It seemed that the whole school was running in the direction of the shouts that grew louder and louder.

Greg reached the stairwell in time to see a police officer and teacher dragging a black student Greg didn't recognize down the stairs. Other teachers and police were hovering over a white student sprawled on the stairs. Then Greg saw it.

The white student's shirt was soaked with blood. An equally bloody knife lay on a stair nearby. The white student had been stabbed.

The entire school dissolved into chaos as students realized what had happened. Quickly, teachers began interspersing themselves among students, dividing whites and blacks, urging students back to their classes. But the situation was already out of control. As if on a signal, white and black students went after each other wildly, kicking, screaming, biting. Teachers and police tried desperately to separate students, yelling at white students to get out of the building, and at black students to go to their homerooms.

Slowly, the fighting students broke up. Most of the white students finally obeyed the order to leave the building. Greg, however, had a white football player pinned in a headlock when a policeman lowered his nightstick on Greg's head. Greg slumped against the wall, stunned, but he noticed through a blur other police officers preparing to carry the stabbed student to a police car. Laurie sat crying on the stairs nearby.

"Oh, God, Jimmy, Jimmy, Jimmy . . . ," Laurie sobbed. The officers finally pushed her to the side and carried the bloody, limp body out to a waiting police car.

Laurie slowly walked down the corridor toward the front door. By the time she hit the front steps, her walk had turned into a run. Sobbing, she joined her classmates who were alerting the neighborhood about the stabbing.

"Come on, man, back to homeroom," said his friend Mel, as he took Greg's arm helping him to his feet. "If that kid kicks over, there's really gonna be some heavy trouble."

"Who is he? Who did it? What the hell happened?"

"I don't know what happened. Just all of a sudden these two guys were going at it, and zap, the dude pulled a knife. Guess he had enough of the mother."

"But who was it? I didn't recognize the guy the cops were dragging away."

"Dunno," said Mel. "But I do know the honky. He's been asking for it. Only a matter of time."

The loudspeaker crackled, and a nervous voice ordered all black students to the auditorium.

As Greg walked into the auditorium, he noted how few black students there were in the school that day: only about a hundred. Now they all seemed very subdued.

"You're probably all aware of what has happened," said the headmaster grimly, as he stood in front of the students. The faculty stood at the back. "A white student has been stabbed. We're going to close the school for the rest of the day. We've called for the buses, but they're still completing the runs for the elementary students. It'll take them another thirty minutes."

Greg looked around him. He knew what the other students were thinking. As if things hadn't been bad enough before, now the white students and Southie itself would feel they had a legitimate right to treat the black students like dirt. It would be open season on blacks.

In the small kitchen of her parents' home, Laurie was telling her mother and some neighbors what had happened at the school. As she told the story, the description of the blood and of Jimmy's condition grew more elaborate. Seeing that Laurie was still upset, her mother tried to soothe her.

"Forget it; you are never stepping foot back in that school while those animals are there," said her mother, clutching Laurie close to her. "Imagine, send a child to school today, and they get stabbed. The more I think about it, the more I think Bunny McLaughlin is right."

Laurie looked at her mother unbelievingly. She had fought with her mother so many times about the Mc-Laughlin family. Sherry McLaughlin was Laurie's best friend. When busing started, Sherry's mother took her three kids out of the public schools and announced they'd go to private school. But even though Sherry's father had a good job with the city, there still wasn't enough money for private school. So Sherry's mother, who had never had a paying job in her life, went to work at a local nursing home, making thirty-eight beds a day to bring home fifty-six dollars a week for her kids' education.

The kids were still at home, because there wasn't yet enough money for the tuition. Mrs. McLaughlin said everything was all right, however, because the kids were being tutored once a week at the Veterans of Foreign Wars post.

Laurie had always thought Sherry's mother had done the right thing — not risking her kids on what Mrs. McLaughlin called a social experiment. But Laurie's mother had taken the stand that her family was not going to be pushed out of their neighborhood school.

"Do you mean it, Ma? I don't have to go back, ever?" asked Laurie anxiously.

"I'll have to talk to your father, but I know he isn't sleeping nights either. And after today . . . well, we'll just have to find the money, somehow." Laurie's mother looked toward the ceiling, shrugging. The neighbors in the kitchen joined her sighs.

At that moment, Mr. Peterson, a neighbor, poked his head through the door.

"Come on, we're all going up to the high school. We're going to find out how they're going to protect our kids. We warned them this would happen."

Laurie's kitchen emptied quickly. When the group was still a block from the school, Laurie realized Mr. Peterson and her mother were not the only parents angry over the stabbing.

The entire area around the school was jammed with people. There must have been five hundred, though the stabbing was less than an hour old.

Laurie grew more frightened. She had never seen so many angry, upset people. The word was that Jimmy was not going to live. Not just students, but parents and grandparents were shouting at the school, "Murderers! Murderers!" "Revenge! We want revenge!"

Just then, several columns of police officers in riot gear began marching toward the crowd from a side street. Officers in front shouted, "Clear the streets! Clear the streets! We've gotta get these buses through."

Laurie watched as the crowd refused to budge. Men and women locked arms, shouted at the police, insisted they would not move. Suddenly it hit Laurie that the black students were still inside, and this crowd was not going to let them out. She watched as people on the steps of a house across the street made crude signs. One of them read "An eye for an eye."

Inside, Greg and his fellow students could hear the commotion on the streets. The time for the buses to arrive had come and gone. Every once in a while a black student would get up and walk into one of the classrooms to look out the window. He would come back and report to the students on how large the crowd was and how many police officers were there.

"Now I don't want everyone getting nervous," said Sgt. Mitchell, one of the few black policemen assigned to Southie. "We're going to get you out. We're sending for more reinforcements to move the crowd. We're just not gonna take any chances."

"Man, come on. How are a handful of cops gonna protect us from those lunatics?" shouted Greg. "No way!"

"Listen, we get the crowd out of here, move the buses

up, and escort you out. Easy, just trust us. And from now on, everyone stay in this room and stay away from the windows."

Greg sighed and put a friendly arm around Rosalie standing next to him, "Don't worry, maybe we'll get a blizzard and it'll bury them."

Outside, the crowd continued to grow. Laurie was surprised to see her father and some men from the train yards coming up the hill to join the crowd. He asked her if she was all right. She said OK, and he moved on to join a larger group of men.

There was still no final word on the fate of Jimmy. Occasionally, a rumor would circulate that he had died, but someone would always come forward with news from the family that he was in surgery, still alive. There were many rumors flying through the crowd. Stories of rapes, students being beaten up by gangs of blacks, threats by blacks to burn down the houses of certain white students. Laurie didn't know which stories, if any, were true. She did notice the crowd was getting angrier and angrier.

"Kill the Niggers! We Want Revenge!" "Kill the Niggers. We Want Revenge!" The chants continued almost without a pause. Some people in the crowd were still crying, their faces red, covered with tears.

"Maybe now this judge will see this isn't going to work," said Laurie to her mother. "He can't force us to go to school together. Those niggers are animals."

"I know they are, and we're just going to have to hope

the judge comes to his senses and sends those kids out and gives us back our school."

Then Laurie heard a different kind of shout, coming from the back of the crowd.

"Watch it, the pigs have brought the horses."

Laurie saw the mounted police trotting up toward the school. The horses hadn't been in Southie since the demonstrations the first few weeks of school. Now they were back in force. It was proof that the police meant business. Horses had a way of pushing back a crowd better than individual police officers.

"Oh, shit, the dogs, too." Behind the horses came four snarling dogs restrained by tactical police officers.

The show of strength, coupled with additional columns of police officers, only made the crowd angrier. They started shouting at the police. A few older kids threw beer bottles at the horses and dogs.

The police began making a sweep, horses in front, pushing back the bulk of the crowd, the dogs and tactical police officers working back the edges. Motorcycle patrolmen watched the side streets to make sure the crowd did not break off into small angry groups.

When they felt the pressure from the people in front being forced back, Laurie and her mother were in the middle of the crowd. Laurie's mother stumbled and fell to the ground. As Laurie leaned down to help her up, another push from the crowd sent her down again. People nearby helped them to their feet, and Laurie began to cry.

She was mad, but she was also scared. First, Jimmy's stabbing, now this mob of people crushing in on her. In back of her people were throwing rocks and bottles, yelling at the cops. In front of her, one horse stumbled, sending its rider to the ground. More bottles exploded on the ground, as police in riot gear moved quickly to raise both the horse and the rider. More bricks flew through the air over her head. More shouts. The cops began to retreat. The crowd cheered. They had held their position.

Inside, black students read, talked, played cards, and listened nervously to the shouting and the sound of bottles smashing. They had been waiting for almost three hours now.

"This is ridiculous, man," said Greg, walking up to Sgt. Mitchell. "Why don't they just clear the streets. What's wrong with them?"

"It's not that easy. There are over two thousand people out there. They're mad. They won't move. We don't want any of our men or any of them to be hurt."

"But what about us? Come on, man, we didn't do anything," Greg shouted, as several students turned and stared at him. Greg realized he wasn't being his usual cool, easy self, so he shifted gears. "Ah, who cares, anyway. Anyone got any cards for poker?"

The police commissioner stood on the steps of the school with a bullhorn, trying to talk to the crowd.

"We are going to clear the streets. Please go to your homes."

He was greeted with boos and shouts of "Hell, No, We Won't Go!"

Slowly, a figure familiar in Southie began working its way toward the steps. Louise Day Hicks, now a city councillor, considered the mother of the anti-busing movement, had been summoned to calm her people.

As her large frame slowly ascended the steps, the crowd recognized its leader and broke into cheers. Those on the steps made room for this formidable woman with her disappearing chins and large thick glasses. With the aid of police officers who quickly came to her assistance, Mrs. Hicks stood on the top stair and nervously accepted the bullhorn that was handed her.

"It's Louise, Momma, it's Louise," shouted Laurie. "She's gonna join us." The last sweep of the police had failed, and now with the appearance of Louise Day Hicks, Laurie was feeling braver.

"My friends, my loved ones," began Mrs. Hicks. Her words echoed as the crowd calmed down out of respect for its beloved leader. This was the woman who, as a member of the Boston School Committee, had led their fight against busing, their fight against allowing blacks into their neighborhood schools.

"James is still alive," Hicks told her audience. She paused while they clapped and cheered. "But we're not helping James by being here. My friends, you have given the court your message, but now we must go home. We must let the black students out."

The bullhorn began to shake as Mrs. Hicks pulled it from her face.

Laurie, her mother, and everyone around them suddenly began shouting.

"No! No! No! Louise!"

Mrs. Hicks continued to shout into the shaking bullhorn, even though her voice was being drowned by the angry protests of her once-loyal followers.

"There has been enough bloodshed. Please . . . please . . . go home. . . ."

But the crowd would not listen. They shouted louder. Mrs. Hicks grew paler.

"I am going home. Please go home with me."

The answer was a defiant "No!" Then a voice, louder than all the rest, came from the middle of the crowd.

"The Bible says 'An eye for an eye.' "

The man's shout was met by cheers from the crowd.

Mrs. Hicks, her hands trembling, took the arms of police officers, and, with tears in her eyes, headed down the steps, across the school yard, home.

"She has to say that," said Laurie's mother. "That's her duty. But inside, she's cheering right along with us. She knew this would happen."

"Kill the Niggers! Kill the Niggers!" Laurie chanted with the others. She had never been a part of this chant before, even during the early demonstrations. It had always seemed a little too strong. But today it did not stick in her throat. She thought of James. Maybe he was dying. She looked at her mother, struggling against the pressure of the crowd. Her father, raising his fist to the school as he spoke to their neighbors. It seemed like her whole world was coming apart. Her school, her neighborhood.

Now the police were coming toward the crowd in even larger numbers than before. Many people in front were knocked down. The crowd was furious. Rocks, bottles — even shoes — were hurled at the police. People overturned trash cans and threw more bottles and cans. Laurie and her mother were picking up people in front of them as the horses moved in. Hooves and police clubs flashed all around them. Slowly the crowd moved back. Crying. Screaming.

"Why us? Why are you protecting the niggers?" Laurie shouted at the cops. "We didn't do anything. They're the ones who are killing people."

There was no response. The horses and police kept coming. The rocks and bottles continued to fly. Reporters, policemen, parents, and children wiped blood off their clothes.

A few minutes before, in the auditorium, Sgt. Mitchell had told the black students to form a single line. As they were getting into line, several columns of tactical patrol officers marched into the auditorium. They were all in riot gear, with masks, guns, and clubs. They interspersed themselves among the students, standing sometimes every other student, sometimes every two or three students.

Everyone was quiet for a moment as Sgt. Mitchell looked at his watch. He seemed to be listening for something. Soon everyone heard the sounds of renewed fighting between the cops and the crowd.

"OK, this is it, kids. Don't be nervous. We're going out the back door. Down a back walk to the buses. Now we've got plenty of policemen to help you. The crowd is being moved the other way. But they shouldn't even see you. Just be quiet. And move as fast as you can."

Greg immediately understood. It was a fake-out. The cops would keep the crowd busy outside, letting them think the buses were coming up in front any minute. Then the blacks would sneak out the back. Good plan, thought Greg, if it works. It seemed like a gamble. Greg didn't like being a gambling chip.

But there was no time to think about that. Quickly, they went down the stairs, through a basement corridor. Police officers stood by an open door.

"It's all clear, Sergeant. Good luck."

"OK, kids. Move fast and stay quiet."

With that, the race was on. Students and police alike ran out the back door, through the school yard, across the street, through a yard, and down a long flight of steps that ran between the houses of Southie. There was no time to think about the crowd, or to look back. The riot police kept the students moving fast. Sometimes they carried a slow mover by dragging him along.

Even Greg found the pace a little fast for him. It was unfamiliar territory to be running in so fast. But run he did, and at one time he grabbed Rosalie's hand to hurry her up. The only thing he was sure of was that the crowd was still there. He could still hear their chants behind him as they screamed for blood. He could hear the horses, the dogs.

Finally they saw the buses and broke into a final sprint. The police pushed them in. While people were still standing, the buses took off, a police car and motorcycles in front but no siren, no flashing lights.

Greg found a seat on the rocking bus for him and Rosalie. He was breathing roughly and realized his whole body was shaking.

"Jesus, this is a hell of a way to go to school," he sighed. Then it struck him, and he began to laugh.

"Hey, it worked," he shouted. "The honkies are still waiting for the buses to come. Boy are they going to be pissed when they find out we're gone!"

In front of the school the police rush seemed to end as abruptly as it began. The police began pulling back on a signal from the captain. A few people were arrested for assaulting officers. But the crowd stood in amazement as cops began to disperse. The horses and dogs went back to where they came from.

"Hey, what is this? What's going on?" screamed Laurie. "They can't be letting us alone."

Others joined her shouts, and eventually a retreating policeman turned around and shouted at the crowd.

"You can stay here all you want. They're gone. The school is shut down for the rest of the week."

The crowd was stunned. Some people figured out how the students had left, and the crowd grew even angrier.

But there was no one to be angry at anymore. The police were leaving. The black students were gone.

Laurie began to cry again, although she wasn't really sure why. Here she was in the middle of a glass-strewn street on a December afternoon, mad, frustrated. She looked down the street and saw a crowd gathering around a police car. They began rocking it, and, before police officers could break up the crowd, they flipped it over. A cheer went up. Laurie began smiling and joined the cheer.

Christopher and His Father

CHRISTOPHER would always remember the day he received his assignment to the Jeremiah E. Burke High School. It was the same day his father received his tax bill.

"Wish I never opened the damn mailbox!" Mr. Wheeler flung both papers into the corner and stomped into the living room.

"Gonna be able to pay it?" Chris asked from his chair in the corner by the television set.

"Yeah, we can pay it, but I sure don't like it. First the car insurance goes up three hundred bucks! On a three-year-old Chevy! Then they put in a new water commission to save us money, and the water bill goes up a hundred bucks. Jesus, I hope they don't try and save me any more money. I can't afford it!"

"See my assignment to the Burke?"

"I saw it. Forget it."

"I don't wanna go there. It's right in the middle of Roxbury. Has a rotten reputation."

"I said forget it. You're not going there."

"What am I gonna do?"

"You'll go back to Brighton High or something. I don't know, we'll work it out when your mother gets home."

Mr. Wheeler couldn't seem to sit still. He walked to the front door, then to the window, then back to the couch.

"I don't know how they expect people to live in this city! Unless you're workin' and your wife's workin' and you don't buy a new car, and you don't go out to dinner ever, you can't afford to live here. I can see why people are movin' out."

"Reillys are movin' to Quincy."

"See? More every day. The middle-class property owner in this city just can't carry the weight for everyone!" It was a refrain Chris had grown accustomed to in the last few months.

"It's gonna get just like Detroit. All the white home owners are gonna move out and all that's left in the city will be blacks."

Chris turned at the sound of the back door opening. Mrs. Wheeler worked afternoons at the customer service counter at the A&P down the street.

"Hi, Mom. Guess what? Bad news. I got assigned to the Burke."

"I thought that was a school for colored kids," Mrs. Wheeler said as she hung up her coat in the hall closet.

"Used to be. Now they're trying to send whites there too, I guess."

"Why can't you go back to Brighton High? You only got one more year."

"I don't know."

"We'll see about this." Mrs. Wheeler was a thin, feisty woman who preferred to be up and doing rather than sitting and moaning. She moved now to the telephone in the hallway and thumbed busily through the phone book. "I know, for sure, our budget can't take sending you to private school, so we'll have to find another way."

"Oh, that reminds me," interrupted Mr. Wheeler. "We got the tax bill. Up again."

A groan came from Mrs. Wheeler. Mr. Wheeler offered a consoling smile and the inevitable "What can we do?" gesture. He leaned his stocky frame against the wall, and ran his hand through his graying hair. He watched his wife anxiously go through the phone book. He was a clerk for the city's election commission, a job he had come by through his unwavering loyalty to the city's Democratic machine. He had used his connections to snare a summer job in the parks department for Chris. And since her graduation from high school two years ago, Chris's older sister, Marty, had worked for the city full time in the personnel office.

"Hey, Dad, maybe you can talk to someone at City Hall about my school assignment. They can get it fixed."

"We'll see, kid."

Now they both listened to Mrs. Wheeler's side of the telephone conversation.

"Yes, Christopher Wheeler. He went to Brighton High last year, and we just got his assignment to the Jeremiah Burke. I want to find out how to change it." She covered the mouthpiece and said over her shoulder, "They're getting one of the supervisors at the school information center."

She waited.

"Yes, this is his mother. Yes, we just got it in the mail and he can't go there. . . . Because we don't want him to, that's why. . . . We live in Jamaica Plain."

The supervisor put her on hold. Mrs. Wheeler reached for the window curtain near her that needed straightening. She turned her head toward her husband.

"As hard as we've worked, Jim, to get this house, this neighborhood—and now a bunch of strange kids will come into the schools, and Chris is sent into the middle of the ghetto."

She fingered the lace curtains, her eyes roaming over their home. They had moved to Jamaica Plain just four years ago. Before, they had lived closer to the center of the city, but they had wanted their own home, not a three-decker apartment shared by another family. After years of saving and cutting back, they were able to afford a modest house on an ordinary residential street in back of a large open pond. And it was still in the city. Their neighbors were white middle class: some policemen, some office workers, a few businessmen. Like the Wheelers, many families were from less prosperous city neighborhoods and had scrimped for years in order to buy their present homes.

Mrs. Wheeler began tapping her foot on the floor. Her voice grew angry.

"Why can't he go back to Brighton High? He's only got one more year. . . . So if we're not in Brighton High's district, whose district are we in? The Burke." She looked disgustedly at Chris and his father. "Look, we want to transfer, what do we do? Yeah. . . . Yeah. . . . Says who? . . . Drat!" She slammed the phone down.

"What happened?"

"It's all this busing. That judge made up new school districts to bus the black kids into the white schools. So we're not in Brighton's district."

"Why can't I go there anyway?"

" 'Cause you can only go to schools in your district, dummy!" She gave Chris a half-playful whack on the head. "The woman said we could try a magnet high school—you know, one that takes kids from all over the city—but they're all full."

"You mean I gotta go to the Burke? I ain't goin'."

"No one says you're goin'," Mr. Wheeler declared. "Let me see what I can do at City Hall."

Chris followed his mother into the kitchen as his father picked up the phone. Although he was seventeen, Chris was nearly as small and thin as she was. He pushed back the swatch of black hair that kept falling in his eyes.

"If I have to go to the Burke, I'm not goin' at all!" he announced defiantly.

"No one said you have to go. Keep your shirt on, will you? Jesus!" She paused. "Just one more year to go. We have all the luck. At least I didn't have to go through this with your sister." Marty had ridden the bus halfway across town every day to graduate from Brighton High.

"Aren't there colored kids at Brighton?" she asked.

"Sure there are. Not as many as whites, but there are plenty."

"So what does that damn judge want? You were already goin' to school with coloreds, or blacks, or whatever."

Mr. Wheeler walked into the kitchen. "No go. Jack says there's nothing he can do. Says he's been swamped with calls, and if he could help anybody out it would be me. But it's out of his hands." He slumped into a chair at the kitchen table.

"You know, I just don't understand all this. Here you've got a kid going into his last year at an integrated school. An integrated school! And a good one at that! So you take him and tell him he's gotta go to one of the worst schools, in one of the most dangerous parts of the city, where he'd probably be the only white kid going!" The three sat silently for a minute.

"It really makes me mad," said Mr. Wheeler, his fist coming down on the table. "When that black family moved in down the street, who told everybody to live and let live? Me! When the anti-busing crazies had their march, who said ignore them, they're only trouble makers? Me. You go along; then you get kicked in the teeth. Paying the highest taxes in the country and now they say send your kids to the worst school in the city." He shook his head, bewildered.

"I'm going to that meeting tonight!" he said suddenly.

"What meeting?"

"Jack says some parents are getting together over on Howard Street. I wasn't gonna go, but dammit, I'm goin'."

"Me too," said Chris.

The living room was hot and smoky: too many people crammed into too small a space. They sat on the furniture, the floor, even the stereo speakers. Some spilled into the next room.

Chris knew a lot of them, people like his own parents. Most of them lived around the neighborhood. He knew some of their kids.

"I tell you, if I could afford to, I'd move out of this city right now!" A man Chris didn't recognize was addressing the room. "But who's gonna buy a house around here? Who's gonna move into my house when they know if they do they give up the right to say where their kids are goin' to school?"

"That's right!" everyone seemed to shout in agreement.

"Let me tell you what this is all about!" Chris looked up in amazement to see his father standing. His father had surprised him just by attending the meeting. Chris had never expected him to speak.

"Here's what this is about! I been workin' for this city for thirty-five, no, thirty-four, years. I'm at my desk every day at nine and I don't leave it until the city has its eight hours outa me. I've done well enough by the city, but it sure as hell hasn't done well enough by me. For eighteen years I worked three nights a week at a truckin' company doin' their books. Not 'cause I'm a workhorse, but because I needed the cash. I wanted a place for my family and not always have to be pourin' out rent."

He gestured to Chris.

"See this boy here? He never got an allowance. He had to work a paper route for his spending money. We all worked. My wife, too. We never got somethin' for nothin'. Nobody ever came up to us and said, 'Here, this is yours because you're white.' "

Several in the room murmured in agreement. Chris's father looked around for a minute before continuing quietly.

"And I never kicked up a fuss. When I thought the taxes were too high, I paid them anyway. Even when the sewers backed up and the streetlights went out and the cops were never around, I didn't bellyache. But now look at this." He gestured at Chris again. "All I can give this boy is a good family and a good start in life. That's all. Nothin' fancy.

"That judge, he sends his kids to expensive private schools. Even the mayor. He don't send his kids to public school, no sir! But me, that's all I got. I can't afford nothin' else. High school is all my kid is gonna get right now. He's not goin' to expensive colleges and all. So what does this judge do? He tells me I gotta take my kid and send him to the worst school in the city in the filthiest, most dangerous neighborhood! You think he's gonna send his kids there? No, sir. And, by Christ, I'm not sendin' mine, either."

The room was silent for a moment after Chris's father sat down. Then people began clapping loudly. Two men came over and slapped him on the back.

When the noise subsided, Jack Flaherty, the city councillor presiding over the meeting, said, "That's what we all feel, Jim, but I've got the big question. What are we gonna do about it?"

He looked around the room.

"We could join ROAR," someone suggested. Several people groaned.

"Not that," another parent said. "I want to keep my kid in his present school as much as anyone else, but I'm not gonna hook up with them. They're nuts." Chris noticed his father nod in agreement.

"That's right," a woman behind Chris spoke up. "We're reasonable adults who are upset about what the court has done. We're not going to throw rocks at children—black or white—but we don't think the judge fully realizes what he's doing to us."

"So how do we convince him?"

"Can't we just talk to him, explain to him how it is?" Chris suggested eagerly, immediately shrinking back in his chair when he saw the people around him smiling at the suggestion.

"If that's all it took," Jack Flaherty said, "I would have

done it years ago. Straightened that damn judge right out. Then I'd be mayor today!" He laughed at the reference to his unsuccessful bid for that office a year ago.

"Now just let me get this straight, Jack," Chris's father leaned forward to speak to the city councillor. "This judge has the power to order me to send my kid to a school five miles away even if there's a school right down the block?"

"Right."

"Even if the school my kid is attending is integrated?"

"Right."

"And his new school will be mostly black and not integrated?"

"Right."

"And that's because, apparently, black kids haven't been gettin' a fair education. That's how he justifies this?"

"Right."

"So he wants me to send my kid to that school where there's no education?"

"Right."

"What happens if I say no?"

"You gonna send your kid to private school?"

"Nope."

"Or some parochial school?"

"Nope."

"You're in trouble then, because the only school you can send him to in Boston is the one the judge tells you to send him to."

"That's like Communism or something."

Flaherty shrugged. "Don't blame me, Jim. I didn't write the court order. I'm only here to help you figure out what to do about it."

"Sounds to me like there's nothing we can do about it," a man in the back of the room shouted.

"Sounds that way to me, too. Come on, Chris, let's get goin'."

Chris stood up and looked awkwardly around the room. Few people looked directly at him. Some stared dejectedly at their hands. Others muttered angrily under their breath. Chris felt a wave of sadness. He hated to see his neighbors get kicked like this and not know what to do to fight it. He couldn't think of anything either.

The late summer night was warm and clear. Chris had to hurry to keep step with his father who was striding along, his hands stuffed in his pockets.

"What are we gonna do?"

"I don't know, kid. I just know this isn't my idea of the American way."

Chris scooted along the bus seat, trying to avoid a rip in the plastic cushion, afraid it might snag his pants. He slid over to the window and dropped his notebooks onto the seat beside him. He didn't know anyone else on the bus and was shy about having anyone sit next to him.

He saw a girl across the aisle look quickly away when he glanced toward her. Maybe they'd get to know each other better as the year wore on.

Chris fingered the corner of his notebook nervously. He

didn't like school much anyway, especially the first day. More than any other first day of school, this one was going to be hard on him.

He rehearsed his lines carefully.

The line at the registration desk grew shorter and shorter. Any minute now it would be his turn to explain why he hadn't enrolled sooner.

"Name."

"Chris Wheeler."

"Address?"

"1145 Parkview."

"Where?"

Chris felt a moment of panic. "What do you mean where?"

"North Quincy or South Quincy?"

"Oh, South Quincy."

"Why are you registering late?"

"I just moved here to live with my aunt."

The clerk looked up at him suspiciously. "You from Boston?"

Chris nodded, a tight knot squeezing his stomach. He hadn't been warned about questions like this.

"My aunt already came down and filled out all the papers."

The clerk shook her head.

"OK, go to homeroom."

Chris looked at his stamped registration papers with relief. He had just enough time to call home. He went to the pay phone by the door and dialed Boston City Hall. He asked for his father in the election commission.

"Hi, Dad, everything went OK."

"Good, good, how do you enjoy suburbia?"

"OK, I guess."

"The school look OK?"

"Yeah."

"How's the bus ride?"

"I'll get used to it."

"Listen, just remember, you're living with Aunt Ruth because of some problems at home. You had to move out for a while. Got it?"

"Sure, I gotta go. The bell's ringing. I think the bus will get me back in time for dinner."

"You're gonna log enough miles this year to be an astronaut." His father's voice sounded tired. "And don't worry, you'll still have time to spend with your friends. And you'll make some new ones." His father sighed.

"Hey, Dad, bet you never thought you'd be payin' all those taxes in Boston and end up sending me on an hour bus trip to school in another city?"

"Never did, kid. Never did."

Kevin

SISTER MARIA folded her hands in front of her and bowed her head. Two dozen twelve- and thirteen-year-olds, jammed together in the tiny classroom, did the same. They droned through the familiar prayer together, Sister Maria keeping a sharp eye on the class through half-closed lids.

In the back row, Kevin squeezed his eyes shut and tried to concentrate. He felt Sister Maria was staring directly at him. It had been a long class for him and not a very good one. It was the first day of catechism class, and he hadn't come prepared. He didn't want to be here at all, but since he was going to public school this year instead of parochial school, his parents had insisted.

Kevin and his younger brother Phil would attend the Martin Luther King School weekdays and religious classes at St. Joseph's on Saturday mornings. It was a route many white parents had chosen in the early years of busing, especially lower-income parents in this heavily Catholic city. They didn't like the busing order, but they couldn't afford to do much else, short of boycotting school altogether, a choice only the most committed anti-busers took.

In other years, Roman Catholics like Kevin's parents might have enrolled their children in parochial school if they didn't like the public school system. This year, though, it was more expensive than ever, a hundred fifty dollars per student. Besides, Cardinal Medeiros had ordered the parochial schools closed to all except those who had attended the year before. Catholic schools, he declared, would not become a refuge for people fleeing the desegregation order.

The prayer ended and Sister Maria fixed the class with a firm gaze.

"You may go now," she said. "But I want to warn you that you must come prepared next week." She looked directly at Kevin. "All of you."

Kevin tried to avoid looking at Sister Maria as he and Phil left the classroom and walked into the early autumn sunshine. Regular schoolwork wasn't easy for Kevin and he didn't look forward to doing more homework for Sister Maria.

He hoped things would go better for him at the King School than they had last year at the Cleveland. He had had so much trouble with geometry and reading that he was being held back. In a few days he and Phil would be entering eighth grade together even though he was thirteen and Phil was a year younger.

"Glad we don't have *her* every day," Phil said as they started up Dana Street toward home.

They walked slowly past the large white house on the corner with its boarded-up windows. Wooden signs nailed to the front announced that the city now owned this house and police would take action against trespassers.

Kevin remembered when the Sullivans lived here. They had eight kids, two dogs, and a hamster. The house caught fire one weekend when they were on vacation, and they never came back. Two nights later, Kevin and Phil looked out of their bedroom window and saw men carrying toilets and sinks out of the house. Their father said it wouldn't be long before someone came and stole the pipes. Three days later those were gone, too. Vandals had even tried to rip out the storm-window frames after they threw rocks through the glass.

Now the house stood boarded up and gutted. Just like the one two doors away. Kevin's father said that's what always happened when a neighborhood was on the way down. He used to tell them what Dorchester was like when the Irish first settled here.

Once families with comfortable incomes had lived here on the huge southern flank of the city. After the war, when money was easier to come by, they moved out, usually to the suburbs. Their large homes were subdivided into apartments and rented to working-class families who couldn't afford to buy their own homes. Usually the landlords lived far away and were seldom seen on Dana Street.

Some of the houses had started to deteriorate badly from neglect. Although the tenants would complain to the landlord, and then to the city, nothing much was done. Water pipes broke, windows cracked, porches rotted, and nothing was fixed. Finally the tenants would move in disgust. Often, only a few nights later, the building would burn. Unless police assigned a man to guard the burned building, and they rarely did, vandals soon would swoop down on the house and strip it of anything that could be sold. If the taxes weren't paid, the city would take it over, and there it would sit: an empty shell looking out onto the street with boarded-up eyes.

Kevin's father predicted that no one would ever buy those houses once they were in that condition, and so far he was right. No one would buy their house, either. Although their block of Dana Street was a short one, theirs was the only house still intact. The house on the corner and another one across the street were already boarded up. Ones around the corner were OK, but it seemed that the neighborhood changed more each week, and it wouldn't be long before there would be boarded-up houses there, too. Kevin worried about what would happen to his family then.

Kevin and Phil walked through the front gate, slammed at the hinge that was always loose, and stopped to check the tomatoes growing in the front yard. The front yard was tiny, as was the house itself, and this year their mother had dug up all the grass and planted tomatoes. "You can't eat grass," she said.

"Let's go down to Columbia Road and skateboard," said Phil.

"Sure," Kevin said nervously. He didn't like to seem scared in front of his younger brother, but Columbia Road made him nervous. It was one of the dividing lines between white Dorchester and black Dorchester. On his side of Columbia Road there were no black families. On the other side of Columbia Road, there were no white families. The King School was just on the other side of the road. It was supposed to be a tough neighborhood with tough black kids. Kevin had never been there, even though it was only six blocks away. Phil rode his bike through there once on a dare, and he had said some black kids started to chase him.

Kevin and Phil had a routine. They always skateboarded down a long sloping sidewalk as far as Heller's Pharmacy on the corner. Then they'd turn around and walk back to the start for another run. Kevin enjoyed skateboarding more than most activities, mainly because he felt that he was good at it.

When he shoved off, he could see Heller's four blocks away. He liked to watch it grow closer and closer. Traffic streamed by Kevin as he sailed down the sidewalk, the skateboard bumping rhythmically over the cracks.

As he neared the bottom, he noticed Mr. Heller for the first time. The gray-haired pharmacist was standing outside his store talking to a stout black woman. It was unusual to see many black people on this side of Columbia Road.

He bumped to a stop almost at their feet and was just turning to start up again when Mr. Heller grabbed him by the arm.

"Here's one of your new ones now," he said to the black woman. "Kevin, I want you to say hello to Mrs. Williams. She's the principal at the King School. I just was telling her you and your brother would be two of her new charges. I also told her that you were good boys," he teased, "so don't make a liar out of me!"

Kevin glanced up at Mrs. Williams, who stood watching him calmly, her plump arms folded in front of her. This was the first black woman he'd ever met. He couldn't think of anything to say.

"Hi," he finally mumbled. Mr. Heller was about to urge him into further conversation when Phil jumped off his skateboard a little unsteadily and joined the group.

"I know who you are. You're our new principal. I saw your picture on TV when they were doing a story on the King School."

As Phil rambled on, Kevin took a step back. He was anxious to impress Mrs. Williams because he wanted to do well at the King, but he felt more and more left out as the other three talked among themselves. In a way, though, he was relieved, because he still couldn't think of anything to say.

"I'll see you bright and early Thursday morning," Mrs. Williams said as Phil finally turned to leave. "And you, too, Kevin," she said suddenly, touching his shoulder. "I want to get to know you, too."

Kevin was surprised and pleased. He mumbled a good-bye as he and Phil slung their skateboards over their shoulders and started the long climb up the hill.

Once home, they found several of the neighborhood kids sitting on their front steps where their mother was talking to a few of her friends. Almost none of the other kids on the block were going to the King when school opened. Some had enrolled in parochial school. Others had gone to live with relatives in the suburbs. Some had told the suburban schools they were living with relatives there, but actually they were living at home in Boston and commuting to the suburban schools.

Phil quickly won the attention of the group and re-counted their meeting with Mrs. Williams. "I think she's a pretty nice lady, and everything's gonna be OK," he concluded.

"Good luck to you and the Boston Red Sox," one of the neighbors replied. "They were saying on the news tonight that the King is targeted by the cops as a place where there might be some trouble."

The King's reputation had long been its own worst enemy. For years before the busing order, the King had had an all-black enrollment. It suffered no more violence than any other school, and less than some, but the tattered neighborhood surrounding the school and the shabby appearance of the old brick building itself were enough to brand the King as an undesirable spot.

In many ways, court-ordered desegregation was a boon to the King. With white students about to attend classes there for the first time, the school department suddenly ordered a face-lift for the building after neglecting it for years. New paint and freshly waxed floors brightened the interior, but the neighborhood outside remained the same: very poor and very black.

White parents who were willing to send their children into what they considered reasonably safe black neighborhoods were reluctant to let their children travel through the neighborhood near the King. In this first year of busing, especially, the King seemed a forbidding, mysterious fortress to Kevin instead of a tired brick building six blocks from his house.

At first Kevin lay in bed trying to remember why this was a special day. Then it all came back to him at once; it was the first day of school and it was time to get up.

"You all set?" his mother asked as he came into the kitchen. With four children to get off to school, she usually didn't have much time to talk to anyone. And today she was perhaps more curt than usual, feeling, but not admitting, that she was somewhat uncomfortable with her decision to try the King. She was cast as a maverick in the neighborhood, a role to which she was totally unaccustomed. Most days Kevin didn't mind her preoccupation. Today he wished she would talk more.

Phil was already at the breakfast table, tipping his bowl to scoop out the last bites of cereal. "Come on," he urged Kevin. "We got to get going."

Kevin stuffed down his cereal as Phil kissed his mother

good-bye. As Kevin was saying his quick good-bye, he caught a glimpse of Phil walking out the front door. When he finally caught up with him at the bus stop, Kevin was surprised to see they were the only ones there.

"Think everybody else walked?" he asked Phil.

"You crazy? Nobody else is going."

Just then the school bus rounded the corner and Kevin stretched his neck to see if there were any other white kids on it. As it stopped in front of them, he noticed a girl looking forlornly out of a back window. Between her and the driver there was nothing but empty seats.

"You guys my only customers?" the driver asked.

When they nodded, he slapped the door shut behind them and eased into first gear.

The familiar houses in their neighborhood looked funny when Kevin watched them from the bus window. It was like seeing them for the first time. They seemed older and shabbier than he would have thought.

Scarcely a minute had passed before the bus was on Columbia Road, crossing that invisible line between white Dorchester and black Dorchester. To Kevin, it seemed as if they were entering another town altogether, not just another neighborhood right next to his own. There were almost no yards or trees. Most of the houses were three-decker apartments instead of the one- and two-family houses he was used to. The sidewalks were cracked and dirty, and old newspapers lay matted together in the gutters.

Kevin was surprised to see the sidewalks filled with

kids. They were laughing and joking, paying no attention to the yellow school bus with its three passengers. On this side of Columbia Road, apparently, everyone was going to school.

When the bus stopped in front of the King, a black man jumped on.

"Hi, kids. Welcome to the King. I want you guys to go right into the school by the front door. There's lots of cameras and lots of cops and other folks" — he glanced at the anxious look on Kevin's face — "but there's no trouble! Only a bunch of people who want to make sure it stays that way."

When Kevin got off the bus, he realized what the man meant. There was one group of reporters and cameramen across the street. Apparently they weren't allowed any closer. Next to the bus stood a group of ministers and priests, laughing and talking to each other. And nearly half a block away at the school's side entrance he saw a large number of black kids milling around as a woman did her best to shoo them in the side door.

"Why are they keeping the black kids down there and making the white kids go in the front?" he asked Phil as they climbed the steps.

"So if there's any trouble the whole world doesn't see it, I guess."

Once inside, the two boys were met by a woman who asked them their names then looked at a long sheet of paper. They would be in different homerooms. This was something Kevin hadn't thought of, and it was something that made him a little more nervous. He really didn't like the idea of having Phil in his class because he might not do too well, but it would have been nice to have his brother in the same room on the first day.

An aide whose job it was to help new students get around took each boy to his homeroom. Walking down the corridor, Kevin felt lonelier than he had ever felt in his life. Phil had sauntered off in another direction without even a good-bye.

Now the aide was guiding Kevin past little groups of black kids who were joking and chattering to each other. It seemed that everyone knew everyone else except Kevin, and he didn't know anybody.

"Kevin!" He spun around surprised to hear his name. It was Mrs. Williams, looking very rushed as she moved toward him. "I'm so happy to see you. You have a good day, now, and stop in and see me when you have a chance."

It made him feel good to think the principal would remember him and invite him to come and see her, although he didn't think he ever would.

His classroom was nearly filled with eighth graders buzzing to each other. They hardly glanced at him when he walked in, and he found a seat at the back of the room.

There were about thirty-five kids in the class and Kevin counted only seven white kids including himself. He sat staring at his desk top and listening to the black kids around him greet each other. He felt more and more uncomfortable when he realized he didn't understand some of the words they used, some of their expressions. No one made any effort to talk to him, or, he thought, to the other white kids.

A white boy sitting diagonally across from Kevin suddenly leaned over to him and said, "I ain't comin' back to this place. Are you? They told my mother it was supposed to be fifty-fifty black and white."

"Can we help it if your fifty didn't show up?" a black student asked.

"Yeah, why don't you run home and ask momma about that?" another taunted him.

"Ah, leave 'em alone," another black kid said, and the group returned to its discussion, again ignoring Kevin and the other white kids.

The teacher walked in and ordered the class quiet.

"I'm Ms. Leonard," she began. "I am your homeroom teacher and your math teacher. I've taught at the King for many years and I have a feeling this is going to be one of the best years.

"Of course, a lot of it depends on you," she smiled. "Your first class is math, so you will stay in this room.

"Let's begin. I'm handing out this test, which we'll take now so I can get some idea of where you all are in your math background."

Kevin's heart sank. He was terrible in math; it was one of the reasons he had to repeat eighth grade. And to have a test the very first day!

He looked at his paper and felt sick. It was going to be a terrible year. He couldn't understand the questions at all. They confused him. He made a few guesses.

"All right now, trade papers with your neighbor in front of you. This test doesn't count and I'm going to read the answers out loud and I want you to score your neighbor's test and then we'll hand them in and I'll look them over later."

Kevin almost grabbed his stomach. To have someone else look at his test! He knew this never would have happened at St. Joseph's. There you always knew the teachers and what the first day would be like. Or at least you knew someone you could ask. There wouldn't be unpleasant surprises there.

Kevin was relieved the boy he was trading with was white. He would hate to have one of these black kids discover how bad he was in math and tell all the other kids.

The teacher began reading the answers. The white kid grading Kevin's paper snorted. A few answers later he muttered under his breath, but loud enough for most to hear, "Jesus." He made loud swiping noises with his pencil across Kevin's paper as each answer was read off. Miss Leonard kept reading. The last answer she announced was 38 percent.

"This guy guessed six percent," the white kid said disgustedly. A few black kids nearby giggled and looked at Kevin. He just stared at his paper and pretended he hadn't heard.

When the bell rang, Kevin took his time getting up and out the door, hoping he would be the last and no one would pay any attention to him. A few of the black kids glanced at him curiously, but they were busy with their own conversations.

He followed the kids in front of him down the hall to his next class and searched the corridors anxiously, looking for Phil. Almost every face was black. Most of the white kids were walking alone or with just one other person.

In English class Kevin was bothered to see that the only seat left was across the aisle from the white boy who had tormented him in math class. Trying to ignore the white kid, he slid into his seat just as the teacher walked in.

The teacher, a black man, introduced himself and handed out reading books. This first day, he said, they would read a story out loud, each taking turns.

Kevin sighed. He was bad at reading, but at least not as terrible as he was at math. He was surprised, though, when the first kid stood up to read. He wasn't much better than Kevin. Neither was the next. In fact, just about every student was stumbling over words. Kevin began to feel the knot in his throat grow smaller. At least if he was bad in math and everyone knew it, he wasn't any worse than anybody else in reading.

When his turn came, he stood up and looked carefully at the words in front of him. The white kid who had given him trouble before muttered, "This ought to be good." A few other kids snickered and Kevin felt his face and neck grow hot.

He started reading as softly as he could. When the teacher asked him to speak up, it made him even more nervous. Every time he paused over a word he couldn't understand, the white kid muttered, "Six percent." The more the other students giggled, the more flustered Kevin became. He felt like crying.

Finally he reached the end of the story and plopped himself down in his chair thankfully.

"Fair enough," said the teacher, "and what's your name?"

"Six percent," the white kid mumbled under his breath. This time nearly half the class laughed and looked at Kevin.

He couldn't take it any longer. Kevin slid from behind his desk. He hurled his reading book and caught the white kid square in the face.

"Just stop it!" Kevin shouted at him. "Just leave me alone!"

Kevin noticed a tiny stream of blood running down the boy's chin. His hand was clutched over his mouth and he looked like *he* was about to cry this time. The class watched in shocked silence as the teacher grabbed Kevin by the arm and rushed him out of the room.

The bench outside Mrs. Williams's office was old and hard and uncomfortable. Inside, he could hear Mrs. Williams and his mother talking, but he couldn't understand what they were saying. The teacher had already been in there and left. Next to him, two black kids sat staring at the wall in front of them.

The office door opened and Mrs. Williams told Kevin to enter. He sat down in a chair in front of her desk, several feet from his mother, who looked at him silently.

"What's the matter, Kevin?" Mrs. Williams asked.

"I don't know."

"You don't like it here."

"Nope."

"Why not?"

"I just don't."

"Can't you give it a chance? You don't know anyone yet, and no one knows you."

"It won't make any difference. Not with these kids."

"The black kids?"

"Yeah."

"What about the white kids?"

"Them too."

"What do you suggest then, Kevin?"

"I just don't think I should go to this school. I don't fit in."

His mother spoke for the first time. "We've been over this, Kevin, and there just isn't any choice. You've got to give it a try. We all have to."

"Yeah, I know." Kevin looked down at his hands resignedly.

His mother watched him, then impulsively stood up and crossed the small room to sit next to him. She put her arm around his shoulders.

"Honey, you've just got to try. Please. Just try to hold your temper."

"Yeah, OK."

"Why don't you wait outside for me. I'll be right along."

Kevin left the principal's office and headed down the corridor toward the front door. As he walked down the steps, he could hear the final bell ringing behind him. Soon the street was filled with black kids streaming around him. They didn't seem to notice him any more out here than they had inside.

"This is my brother, Kevin." Kevin turned to see Phil walking up to him, a black boy in tow. "This is Russell." He nodded at the boy. "We're doing our science project together."

Kevin felt even more left out. He was glad when Russell had to leave.

"How'd it go?" Phil asked.

"Rotten."

"Yeah? How come?"

"Got in a fight."

"You're kiddin'." Kevin never got into trouble like this. "With a black kid?"

"Naw. A white kid. Ma's in there." He gestured toward the school.

"Whew. Who won?"

"Nobody."

"Fight in my class too. Two black kids. Just started callin' each other names and stuff. No big deal."

"I don't wanna go here."

"I do. I like it."

"Ma won't let me transfer."

"This is a good school. Too bad more white kids won't come here." Phil looked around at the old school building and the tattered neighborhood around it. "You know what your problem is?"

"What?"

"You just don't like school, no matter where it is." They leaned against a fence and watched the school in silence, waiting for their mother.

"That's not my problem. My problem is school just doesn't like me."

Kim

KIM CHOW leaned her elbows on the seventh-story windowsill and mechanically counted the cars whizzing by on the turnpike below. One out of every ten cars was usually a foreign make, she had noticed one day several years ago. Now whenever she was trying to pass the time, she went to the window and fell into her mental game.

The city looked almost pretty in the late afternoon sun — if she looked straight ahead, that is. Sometimes she would do just that — stare straight in front of her and pretend that's what her neighborhood looked like. The great green trees of Boston Common peeked over the rooftops, hinting at the wide expanse of green below. The common, a large grassy park in the middle of the city, was one of Kim's favorite spots. The new John Hancock Building towered majestically in the distance, reflecting the passing clouds in its glass sides. Vapor trails from airplanes floated lazily on the horizon.

Then the bubble would break. Sometimes music from one of the strip joints two blocks away would do it. Kim sighed. Chinatown just wasn't the neighborhood it used to be.

Chinatown had once stretched for several solid blocks in each direction. It had never been a big part of Boston, but it had been a closely knit, solid community. Then the turnpike was built, eating up much of the district, splitting the rest in half. A few years later, a university expanded its medical school into Chinatown. But the most divisive blow was also the most insulting. An adult-entertainment district had grown up next door to Chinatown. Filled with porno shops, peep shows, prostitutes, pimps, and muggers, it was properly called the "Combat Zone."

As any kid in Chinatown knew by the time he or she was in kindergarten, that meant row after row of dirty book stores, X-rated movies, nude dancing bars, and the prostitutes and drug pushers who fed off such business.

"You know what makes it all worse?" Kim's mother used to say.

"What?"

"The city *wants* the Combat Zone here."

"Why would they want it to be anyplace?"

"No, that's the whole idea. The city decided to put all the dirty book stores and dirty movies and whatnot in one area and not allow them anyplace else. That's a fine idea," she snorted, "if it's not next to your neighborhood!"

"Why don't we get together and do something about it? You know, complain to the mayor or something."

"Ha! You know what it would take to get Chinatown to protest anything? 'Just go along and do your work, don't cause trouble if you don't have to.' That's what people say. Your father, too."

Kim's father and his two brothers ran a small restaurant in the heart of Chinatown. They'd started it right after World War II when the three of them arrived from Canton, China. Now, thirty years later, it was still a small restaurant, making just enough to support the three families.

Kim, who was fourteen, chopped vegetables in the restaurant kitchen on weekends. All of the older children in all three families had worked there at one time or another, waiting on tables, washing dishes. The menu was in English and Chinese, but everyone spoke Chinese in the kitchen.

"Why is everybody here so scared of making waves?" Kim would often ask her mother in frustration.

"Because they've had a hard time in their lives. The older Chinese anyway. Look, many of them still don't speak English, or not very well. That makes you hesitant about marching down to City Hall and demanding your rights. A lot of people here don't even like leaving Chinatown. They're scared." Kim's mother saw the community with the eyes of an outsider. She was French Canadian and would never fit comfortably into the Chinese community regardless of how long she lived in Chinatown. It didn't seem to bother her, though. Kim and her six brothers and sisters considered themselves Chinese.

"People here are proud, too," her mother would say. "Don't forget that. The last time I can even remember a really big community meeting was at least ten years ago. You don't remember, but there was this gang of Chinese boys terrorizing people. Robbing them. They were roaming all over Chinatown. That was bad enough. But then they started branching out. Rolling drunks on the common. Picking pockets downtown. It got in the papers and people here were furious at them. They gave everybody here a bad name. Remember, you make people afraid to come into Chinatown and you make them afraid to come into our restaurants."

"So what happened?"

"So there was a big community meeting and people stood up and yelled about it."

" 'Cause they were scaring away business?"

"That, and the fact that we like to think of ourselves as being able to handle our own problems. If these boys couldn't be controlled by the community, they'd have to be controlled by someone from the outside. The police, probably. And that would be insulting to us. We think of ourselves as strong family people."

"So what happened?"

"So a committee of Chinese leaders went and talked to the boys and their parents. I don't know what they said, but that was the last we heard of any gangs."

"Last we heard of anybody getting together to do anything around here, either."

Now, as Kim looked over the city, she thought of how

much should be done. Chinatown seemed grimy and cramped. Even the telephone booths, which were supposed to be cute because they were shaped like little pagodas, were chipped and peeling.

Kim sighed. She supposed nothing would ever get much better here. She turned from the window and looked at her school books scattered across the kitchen table. School was only two weeks old and already she was up to her ears in homework. She'd better get at it.

Kim and her brother, thirteen-year-old Kenneth, stood on the dusty street corner with a dozen other Chinese students, waiting for the bus to Charlestown. Kenneth yawned.

"Up late doing your homework?" She knew he was watching "Kojak" the night before.

"I wish." Kenneth rubbed his neck sleepily. "I better not get called on in math today. Or in Miss Chen's class."

Kim nodded sympathetically. After a full day at Charlestown, they would return to Chinatown for two hours of Chinese school. Most of the kids from Chinatown attended. They learned to write and read Chinese, even though many of them had picked it up at home from their parents. It was a long day.

"Where's that bus?" Kim craned her neck. She was startled when an unfamiliar voice behind her spoke to her in Chinese. She spun around. A woman she didn't recognize was standing behind them, a girl about Kim's age next to her.

"Are you going to Charlestown?" the woman asked in Chinese.

When Kim nodded, the woman motioned to the girl. "Can you take my June with you? She doesn't know anybody here yet."

"Sure," Kim said. "I'll be happy to." She turned to June. "Are you in the tenth grade, too?" The girl just stared at her and Kim rephrased the question in Chinese.

"Yes," June said in Chinese. "At least I'm supposed to be. We only moved to Boston a week ago. We're staying with my grandparents while my father looks for work."

"Does he speak English?"

"No."

Kim shook her head. He would have a hard time finding anything. One of the small businesses in Chinatown might take him on to wash dishes or to run the presses in the laundry, but he wouldn't make much at all. Not enough to live anyplace but in the projects. Kim felt sorry for June.

"Here's the bus. Come on, you can sit with me." June took her place obediently next to Kim. "Do you know any of the city?" Kim asked, still speaking Chinese. June shook her head.

"This is the Combat Zone. Crummy. Never get caught here at night. It's very dangerous." They passed the blocks of pornographic bookstores and X-rated films in silence. "This is Boston Common. Pretty, huh?" Kim admired one of her favorite slices of the city. People sat on the grass, reading their morning papers. In one corner, a trio of musicians had struck up a song, hoping to collect spare change from passers-by. A vendor was already selling hotdogs.

"That's pretty." June gestured toward the streets lined with gracious townhouses and old-fashioned gaslights they were now entering.

"Beacon Hill," Kim explained. "It's the home of the original Boston Brahmins."

June looked at her blankly. Kim laughed. "You know, the blue bloods! The proper Boston society people! Here's where they live." She pointed to the lovely brick town-houses and well-dressed Beacon Hill matrons walking their dogs on the narrow, winding streets. They hardly seemed to notice the historic landmarks dotting the hill.

"See up there?" She pointed up a hill. "Just a few blocks up, the streets are still paved with cobblestones. Can you imagine that? You can walk on the same cobblestones George Washington walked on."

Kim leaned back in the seat, enjoying her role as guide.

"You seem to like this part of the city a lot."

"I feel comfortable here," Kim surprised herself. She'd never really thought it through. "I mean, you see lots of rich Yankees, but you also see black and Asian people. Mainly professional people or students, I guess. But every-body here seems so calm and . . ." she searched for the right word, "dignified, I guess."

"You seem to know a lot about Beacon Hill."

Kim laughed. "I've been riding the bus through here for years."

"To go to Charlestown?"

"That's right. Lots of kids from Chinatown go to Charlestown. Even before the busing order. There's no high school in Chinatown, so we've always been bused someplace."

"Do the white people in Charlestown bother you? My mother heard there was lots of trouble there."

"No. They never bother us. In fact, I think they are kind of proud of having us around. Some of them say it shows they aren't racists."

Kim shook her head, remembering the first day of school two weeks ago. "It was different when the black kids started going there this year, though. Lots of nasty signs and stuff. I felt sorry for the black kids."

"Were the buses stoned?" June looked out the window nervously. They were entering the outskirts of Charlestown.

"No. Nothing like that. The people were madder at the police than they were at us. Nothing like Southie."

"What's Southie?"

"You *are* new in town! Southie is South Boston. All white. Irish. They were the first ones to get busing last year. White kids were supposed to get bused out. Black kids get bused in. But the white kids wouldn't go. And when the black kids came in the first day, most of the buses were attacked. It was terrible."

"So what happened to the black kids?"

"Oh, they're still there."

"What happened to the people from Southie?"

"They're still throwin' rocks at the buses."

"Where are the police?" June looked out the window at their own light police escort, only a few motorcycles.

"There's about an army of them getting the buses in and out each day. But don't worry about it," she reassured June. "There haven't been any problems like that in Charlestown. Like I say, people are mainly fighting with the cops, not us."

June still looked anxious as their bus turned onto a steep hill leading toward the high school. A few street corners had small clusters of curious people, but they were far outnumbered by the police. At the high school itself, there were several dozen police and virtually no one else — only students straggling in.

"See," Kim waved at the high school as they stepped out of the bus. "Nothing to worry about."

"Kim! Kim Chow! Come here a moment!" Kim turned to see one of her neighbors, Mrs. Lee, talking to the headmaster.

"Why, what are you doing here, Mrs. Lee?" Kim knew Mrs. Lee worked as a legal secretary downtown, although she still lived in Chinatown. It was unusual for older college-educated Chinese to stay in Chinatown. Most just wanted to move up and out. Mrs. Lee was widely respected for staying and for working hard in several Chinatown projects.

"I can't go into it now, Kim. Is this the new girl? June? There are several new children this morning, and I want to get everyone straight. Do you speak English, June?"

June looked at Kim in confusion. Mrs. Lee asked the question again in Chinese.

"No," June replied.

"You'll have to stick with her today," Mrs. Lee said to Kim. "But after school, I want you to come to the activity center. Bring June with you. You can skip Chinese school today; I'll explain it to your parents." Mrs. Lee turned back to a heated discussion with the headmaster.

Bewildered, Kim led June into the sturdy old building and to their homeroom.

"She's new today," Kim explained to the teacher, Ms. Binnelli.

"All right, dear, just fill out this form and give it to me at the end of homeroom." Ms. Binnelli handed June a piece of paper and waved her to a chair near Kim's.

Kim stacked her books neatly on her desk top and settled down to hear the morning announcements. Out of the corner of her eye, she noticed June turning the form around and around in her hands.

"Of course," Kim thought, exasperated with herself, "June can't read it."

She raised her hand. "Can I just help June fill this out, Miss Binnelli?"

"Can't June understand English?"

"No, ma'am. She doesn't read English either."

"Oh, dear. Well, you'd better then. And you'd better stay with her today."

In history class, Kim walked up to the teacher, Mr. Benson, right away and explained the problem.

"Well, Kim," Mr. Benson said, "I guess it's OK for you to help her out, but we're spending most of the period today talking about the Civil War. I want you to be taking notes for a paper we're doing next week. How can you do both?"

"Oh, don't worry. I'll manage." Kim led June to a seat next to hers and opened her notebook expectantly. She was especially fond of history.

Suddenly, she had an inspiration. "You take notes, too," she whispered to June. "Do it in Chinese. I'll tell you what's going on." Obediently, June opened her own new notebook.

Mr. Benson began. "As I was explaining yesterday, there were many differences between the North and South in the years before the Civil War. Slavery wasn't the only difference. There were economic considerations as well."

Kim wrote busily in her book. She felt a nudge on her arm and looked up to see June looking at her quizzically.

"What's he saying?" June whispered in Chinese.

"Oh, sorry. I forgot already. He says there were lots of differences between the North and South right before the Civil War. Economic differences, too."

June scribbled in her notebook. "The north and south what?"

"What?" Kim had already turned back to Mr. Benson's lecture.

"The north and south what? What does he mean?"

"North and south states," Kim whispered urgently. Mr.

Benson was moving toward a big map in front of the room. She missed the first few words he said.

"Where?"

"Where what?" Kim answered in exasperation, trying to hear Mr. Benson.

"Where were the north and south states?"

"In the United States! Where else! This is American History!" Kim hadn't realized she'd raised her voice above a whisper. The students near them turned and shushed her. She glanced at June, who had turned back to her own notebook. She was sitting still now, her head bowed over her paper. Kim was sorry she had snapped.

"It's OK," she whispered. "I was just trying to keep up. I'll tell you what he's saying."

June smiled. "Thanks."

Kim turned back to Mr. Benson. He was talking about imports and exports. She had missed the middle part and couldn't figure out where he was.

"I'll just have to get it from somebody else," she thought, a little disappointed, "for both of us."

It was the same the whole day. Kim explained June's language problem to each of her teachers and they all agreed to let Kim translate for her as the class went along.

"The only problems is," Kim thought near the end of the school day, "I didn't get much done myself today." She looked at June and smiled. She didn't want June to feel bad about it. It wasn't her fault.

After school, Kim sat impatiently on the bus, more

curious than ever about Mrs. Lee's mysterious instructions to go to the activity center. The center was part of a new brick housing project in Chinatown. A lot of older people lived there, as well as some families.

So far, the clean red brick was marred only by a few graffiti marks, chalked on in white. The rest of the complex was nearly as clean as it had been when the project opened. If it was one of the cleanest in Boston, it was also one of the safest. Boston's Chinatown had largely escaped the teenage gangs and drug traffic that plagued other Chinese communities, especially the sizable ones in San Francisco and New York. Boston's Chinese leaders were determined to keep it that way.

Kim was surprised to see the activity room nearly filled with people. She spotted Kevin Chung from the mayor's office huddled with Mrs. Lee in what seemed to be an angry exchange of words.

"All right, the meeting will come to order." George Ling of the Chinese Merchants Association was at the front of the room, pounding on a table. Kim pulled June to a seat at the back of the room.

"Mrs. Lee, you have the floor."

"I want to thank you all for coming here on such short notice. But our problem is so urgent that we felt it couldn't wait.

"What we have discovered in the last several days of careful investigation is that many of our young people are suffering badly at school."

The room buzzed with concern. "Not that they're being

physically mistreated," Mrs. Lee explained quickly, "but it's nearly as bad. Many, many children are sitting in classrooms with no idea of what's happening there. As you know, many of our families do not speak English well. Their children are sitting dumbly in class day after day, not participating, not learning."

"They might as well be folding sheets at the laundry," a young man grumbled loudly.

It was John Lu, widely considered a hotheaded young man who spoke more than he listened. Still, he was respected in the community because he worked hard at the Youth Activity Office and because no one questioned his sincerity. His remark had been intended sarcastically, and everyone took it that way. John Lu had long been trying to break young people out of the traditional laundry and restaurant jobs and get them into other work. The Chinese children who attended the prestigious Boston Latin School — and there were a lot of them — went on to college and had no trouble. But most of the others followed their older brothers and sisters into the traditional jobs without thinking much about it.

"It's nearly that bad," Mrs. Lee said, surprising everyone by agreeing. "We had been promised Chinese-speaking transitional aides and bilingual teachers in the classrooms where our children would be. The school department and the city have not come through with either. And, as far as I can see" — she looked pointedly at Kevin Chung — "they don't intend to. What shall we do about it?"

A general buzz broke out again and Kim could see the meeting was about to split into a dozen separate discussions when she heard George Ling pound on the table.

"All right, I have a hand in the front. Only people who raise their hands will be recognized."

It was a well-dressed woman in her early twenties. Kim recognized her as Sharon Lewis, one of the few Chinese teachers at Charlestown.

"Let me tell you from my own experience that this situation is deplorable. In this room, we have a perfect example of what I'm talking about." She gestured broadly toward the back of the room. Kim wondered what she was getting at.

"Kim Chow has spent the entire day showing June Fong around Charlestown High School." Kim blushed in embarrassment as everyone turned around to look at them. "It was no surprise to the school that June was coming, and it was no surprise that her English is not too good. Still, if it weren't for Kim's generosity, she would have understood nothing of her first day in school." Ms. Lewis banged her hands together in exasperation.

"There was not a bilingual class for her to attend and no Chinese transitional aide to show her around. And there won't be, either, if the school department has its way! They'd rather not be bothered. If we don't do something, Kim will spend the rest of her school year doing what the school department should be doing!" Ms. Lewis was angry. Kim had never seen a teacher so angry.

John Lu now got to his feet. For a curious moment he

was quiet. He just looked at his hands. Then quietly, began to talk.

"This school system has never cared about us. They've never paid any attention to us." His voice began to grow louder. "Just like they never paid any attention to the black students. Now they have to pay attention to the black students. But what's going to make the school department help us?"

"But that's the point," said Ms. Lewis. "Everything's out in the open now. The court is watching all minorities, not just blacks. We've got to make sure our voice is heard by the federal court."

"What do you suggest?" someone shouted from the audience.

"We've been cooperative too long," answered Ms. Lewis. "By being peaceful and trusting and not making any waves, we've let them use us!"

The crowd murmured angrily.

Kim sauntered to the bus stop the next morning out of curiosity. The vote to boycott the schools had been unanimous. The Chinese community in Boston, usually so docile, was aroused. Kim knew the boycott would be total. When Chinatown got together in its anger, that was it.

Even though not everyone in Chinatown wanted to miss school, they would stay out once the majority had decided to boycott. Kim watched the bus pull up empty. She was right. The boycott was one hundred percent.

Kim walked back toward her apartment building wondering what to do with herself. She noticed a small clump of people gathered on one of the sidewalks and walked over curiously. A television reporter was interviewing Kevin Chung. Kim knew he would be supporting the boycott, even though he worked for City Hall. When push came to shove, she thought, people knew he would side with the community.

"What we're demanding," Chung explained to the camera, "is the proper support personnel for Chinese students in Charlestown. We want Chinese aides to help the non-English-speaking students through their classes. We want bilingual classes to supplement their regular classes. Until we get what we want, no Chinese students will attend public school. Not in Charlestown, not anyplace else. It's as simple as that."

Kim was proud. She had always resented the way Chinatown was treated. The Combat Zone next door ("They'd never allow that on Beacon Hill," her mother would say), the streets that never seemed to get cleaned, the way the community was continually pulled apart by people from the outside, the racism some Chinese faced if they didn't speak English.

She had been a little envious when the black community pushed its desegregation suit in court. Of course, the black population in Boston was much larger than the Asian, and they were usually treated much worse than the Chinese kids in school. Still, Kim thought to herself, they finally stopped letting people push them around. Now we're going to take a stand, too.

Farther down the block, Kim could see John Lu in the middle of a group, gesturing excitedly. Kim rushed over.

"I tell you," he told his audience, "it was terrific! You should have seen them!"

"Seen whom?" Kim shouted.

"The school department people. They were trying to convince our people to go back to school while they met about this. Everyone said, 'Forget it!'"

"Why do they care if we go to school or not?" an older woman spoke up.

"Because," John said, pleased with his role as an authority, "it looks lousy if they don't do something for us. Here we've been cooperative all along, and they haven't come through with what they've promised. It just looks lousy. Even the papers say so."

Kim nodded in agreement. Never, she thought, had Chinatown gotten so much attention. Sometimes in the past a newspaper reporter or a television reporter would come to Chinatown to do a feature story, but most of the articles came out sounding the same to her. They made it sound as if Chinatown were a strange faraway city instead of one neighborhood in Boston.

One story on television had said, "Chinatown is as inscrutable as its population." That had made John Lu so mad he tried to organize a picket line at the TV station to protest it as a racist story, but he couldn't get many people to go along with him, so the whole idea had fallen apart.

Now, though, Chinatown seemed to be crawling with reporters, and they were all asking questions. Why were the kids out of school? How long would the boycott last? Was it all because of busing?

Kim chuckled when she heard the last one asked. If anything, busing had been a boon to many of the Chinese students. The elementary school in Charlestown was brand new, and their shabby elementary school in Chinatown had been replaced with a handsome new building. Chinatown didn't have enough neighborhood schools for all its kids anyway, so they were used to riding across town to go to school.

"How long has it been now?" Kenneth asked Kim. They were sitting on the broad stone steps in front of the new housing project, passing the time with several friends.

"Four days. Seems longer." Kim scratched at the cement steps with a stick. Staying out of school was more boring than she had expected.

"We won! We won!" John Lu raced around the corner of the project, whooping and leaping in the air in excitement.

"What happened?" Kim was one of the first to rush up to him.

"The school department gave in on everything! Chinese transitional aides! Bilingual classes! Even the court changed its rules so more Chinese parents will be on parents' councils! Can you believe it?"

Kim and her friends pounded John on the back, then turned to congratulate each other. They felt that they had won a big victory. Two older women coming out of the project joined them. Everyone knew how much had been at stake in the boycott.

"This is only the beginning!" John Lu crowed. "Now that we know we can do it, we'll organize for better police patrols and new streetlights! Now they know they can't mess with us!"

Kim shook her head and turned to Kenneth. "You know, he's right, but he's wrong."

"What do you mean?"

"All that stuff should be done," she waved around her at the deteriorating buildings, "but it'll be a long time before people get mad enough to do anything about it again."

"How come?"

Kim shrugged. *"We* liked being interviewed and on TV and all, but do you think the older people liked the limelight?"

"Not a chance. The one time Dad saw a camera coming, he went the other way. I think he's afraid they'll laugh at him because of his English."

Kim nodded. "That's right. And there's more people in Chinatown like him than like John Lu. They just want to go back to business as usual."

Kenneth sighed. "Kind of too bad in a way."

"Yeah, well, I guess John Lu will just have to wait until we grow up to really shake this place up!"

They laughed and headed back for their apartment.

Jerome

CHARLESTOWN WAS READY for its day in history. The year before, when the buses rolled through most of Boston but not Charlestown, many Townies, as the longtime residents liked to call themselves, were a little envious. After all, the sentiment against busing and blacks was just as strong here as in Southie. And the locals wanted a chance to show it.

It wasn't as if Townies did not involve themselves with the trouble in South Boston during the first year of desegregation. The people of Charlestown were like cousins to those of Southie — working-class Irish who lived in modest homes and worked at low-paying jobs. It was a tight, proud community. The year before, many Charlestown residents had rushed to support their friends in Southie by joining anti-busing marches or protests in front of the high school.

But they really wanted to be fighting on their own turf. Now, in the second year of desegregation, their chance had come. This year, blacks were to be bused into Charlestown, whites out.

"Oh, man, are we gonna show Southie how it's done."

Jerome sat with several other white youths on the back steps of the Bunker Hill housing project one night late in August.

"Southie just wasn't tough enough. They let the cops whip 'em. Let the niggers take over their school. That ain't gonna happen here."

A tall, well-built sixteen-year-old with a shock of red hair, Jerome had grown up in the streets of Charlestown. For the last six years, he and his family had lived in the Bunker Hill housing project, a square red-brick project strewn with broken bottles, torn trash bags and crowded by too many people. A cluster of four-story brick buildings, the project squatted at the bottom of Bunker Hill, the historic spot where the Revolutionary army had fought one of its first major battles. If Bunker Hill was a drawing card for Charlestown, the Bunker Hill housing project was a place many wished either would be upgraded or just go away.

Six years ago, it wasn't a bad place to live, and Jerome's father, who worked for a city councillor part time, said he could get a deal that would allow him to live at the project for practically nothing. Today the rent was still cheap, but the place had really gone downhill.

In Jerome's apartment, the bathroom ceiling was shredded and stained yellow-brown from a leak in the apartment above. The tiles around the stove were cracked and curled, and his mother had given up complaining to the housing authority to get them fixed. The whole place smelled funny. Small-scale graffiti decorated the hallways in the building — curlicue hearts with initials inside them, first names and high school graduation dates. "Jerome, '76" was all over the place.

But Jerome didn't care what condition the project was in. His friends were all from the project. He could always find a place to crash, drink beer, smoke dope. And anyway, he was entering his senior year of high school, and then it was going to be off to the Marines. He wasn't even sure if he'd wait until he graduated. His mother and father said he could do what he wanted.

These days his mother was too busy to pay much attention to what he did anyway. She was one of a group of Charlestown mothers who had founded an organization they called "Powder Keg." They hated busing and hated blacks coming into Charlestown. Their organization's name was intended as a warning: if busing came, Charlestown might explode.

"We've got to make sure we get a lot of kids out for the march tomorrow," Jerome burped and reached for another Budweiser. "We get the cameras and reporters over here and shit, bang . . . we let the niggers know right off Charlestown don't want no coons."

"Yeah, but Christ, I'm getting so sick of these damn marches," said Eddie, Jerome's friend. "Let's bring on the real thing!"

"The niggers will be here soon enough," Jerome smirked. "And everybody's going to be sorry."

The squeal of tires racing into the project parking lot diverted the group. It was Jackie, another kid from the project. He was known as a tough guy and had already been in a lot of trouble with the police.

"Hey, come on! We're rattling some of the cops! Bring me a beer."

Eddie and Jerome and two other kids ran over and got into Jackie's car. The slick, polished Chevy took off, leaving as much rubber as it came in with.

They parked in a deserted lot not too far from the housing project's last building and joined about twenty other kids all standing around burning trash barrels.

"Where are the cops? What's the deal?" asked Jerome.

"They keep pushing through on their bikes, trying to get us to break it up to go home," said one of the older guys. Jerome didn't know his name, but he was always hanging around with the older gang of townies.

"Here come the pigs now!" came the warning from a distant voice. They could hear the roar of motorcycles and see the lights of several of them poke through the darkness. As the police drew closer, someone threw a bottle in their direction. It missed its mark and smashed to the side of the police officers. In one quick maneuver, the motorcycles turned from the crowd and headed in another direction.

"Guess they're a little chicken," said Eddie.

"Shit, I was hoping we were going to have some fun tonight," complained Jerome, opening another beer. "I was hoping to practice my aim." He grinned at Eddie. "Those niggers make a tough target, you know."

"Hey, will you punks get out of here!" shouted some-

one from a nearby townhouse. "Go cause trouble someplace else."

"Ah, stuff it, will you?" shouted back one of the older
guys.

As others turned to shout at the voice from the window, a police car approached, followed by a police wagon.

"OK, which one of you guys threw the bottle?" demanded a policeman as he pulled himself out of the car.
"Don't you kids have nothing better to do tonight? I
want you all out of here — now."

"Ain't this a public street?" said Jerome, waving his
cigarette.

"That's right, pal, and you're going to get off of it."
He reached for Jerome, but Jerome pulled back.

There were now several policemen behind the one
talking. They started forward.

"OK, we're going, we're going," said Jerome quickly
as he turned and walked away. He kicked one of the
burning trash cans and shouted over his shoulder, "Just
wait. Just wait."

They squeezed back into Jackie's car, joined now by
several others.

"What the hell is their problem?" Jackie muttered.
"Since when can't we hang on the street?"

"It's because of all this busing crap. They don't want
trouble," said Eddie. "But they're going to get it."

The flap-flap-flap of what sounded like huge wings
made Jerome think he was still dreaming the next morn-

ing. He lay in bed with his eyes shut, barely awake, listening to the strange sound. As he grew more conscious, the sound sorted itself out into a steady whir that regularly got loud, then faded away before it returned louder once again. When comprehension finally struck him, Jerome sat up straight in bed. A helicopter was circling over the Bunker Hill housing project.

"Holy Christ," he muttered as he pulled on his pants and yanked back his bedroom curtains. It was still only six-thirty, but already he could make out the metallic glint from dozens of blue helmets in the street.

He rushed into the living room in time to see his mother disappearing out the front door, her bathrobe flapping and a wisp of cigarette smoke swirling about her.

On the sidewalk, dozens of people were already gathered, some still in their slippers, roused as Jerome was by the helicopter circling closely overhead.

Nearly one hundred police in full riot gear stood in casual knots on the sidewalk across the street from the project.

"Hey, you! Get the hell off my roof!"

Jerome spun around to see his father waving wildly at the roof of their building. It took a moment for Jerome to realize there were two policemen stationed there, each holding a sleek high-powered rifle. Jerome squinted at the skyline, brightening by now, and counted seven other policemen on the rooftops of nearby buildings.

He blinked his eyes in the early morning light and

wondered what had happened to bring out such a massive police showing. Then he realized that nothing had happened — the police just wanted to show everyone they were ready. Jerome remembered two nights ago when his father was watching the television news. A reporter was saying that the police had been embarrassed last year in Southie when they had badly underestimated the opposition to busing there. On the first day of school they had let buses of black kids go into South Boston with no police protection. Most came out with smashed windshields and screaming kids.

Even Jerome was amazed. He had expected the police to pull out the stops once the community got something going. Once they caused some trouble. So far on this opening day of school, no one had done anything. And yet there the police were, watching the project through high-powered lenses, nightsticks and tear gas ready.

"Christ," Jerome thought, "if it weren't for that damned helicopter, I'd probably have slept through opening day."

"What is this, World War Three?" Jerome's mother shouted at the riot-equipped police across the street. She was a stubby woman with straight black hair cropped bluntly at the back of her collar.

"We ain't done nothing, and you got a helicopter and guys with rifles?" She waved her arms angrily at the police, shouting to no one in particular.

Finally, a captain detached himself from the ranks of police and started across the street. Jerome pushed his way to the front of the crowd. Like most teenage boys in the project, he felt it would be disgraceful for anyone to belittle his mother in public, even though they fought a lot at home themselves.

The big police officer came about three-quarters of the way across the street.

"Look lady, you don't do nothin' when those buses drive by today and we'll leave you alone. You cause any trouble and we'll take you in. It's as simple as that." He turned on his heel.

"I thought you guys was on our side!" Jerome yelled over his mother's shoulder. He heard people around him murmur in agreement.

"What's wrong?" he shouted at the retreating back. "You guys all turn into nigger lovers?"

"You used to be Townies, some of you," his mother took up the refrain.

When the captain just kept walking, the crowd broke into disgruntled knots. Jerome paused to spit in the street, then headed toward the corner, where he spotted several of his friends. The whir of the helicopter overhead and the proximity of so many police made him feel excited in a way he didn't entirely understand.

"You believe this?" Eddie asked.

"They're just gonna piss people off more."

"Want to go up to the high school?"

"Yeah, let's see what's happening."

They eyed the police still congregated on the opposite sidewalk and decided to head up Bunker Hill Street and then cut up a side street to the school. Charlestown High sat on a hill right next to the Bunker Hill Monument. A large square building, Charlestown High was old and rundown, in need of modernization.

Compared to the crowds at the housing project, the side streets seemed sleepy and calm. The group sauntered past the houses that were slapped next to each other in typical Boston fashion and crowded right up to the sidewalks. There were front steps to some, but no lawns.

"Which way you think the buses are coming?" someone asked.

"Not too many choices." Jerome stopped to pick up a rock. Half a block up the hill he sorted through a trash can and pulled out a beer bottle. He stuffed it in his back pocket.

They turned a corner and stopped in surprise. Only a half a block in front of them a black boy was walking quietly up the hill, his notebooks tucked under his arm.

"Are you kiddin' me?" Jerome asked in amazement. He reached in his back pocket and hurled the bottle as hard as he could, cursing himself for hurrying as it fell several yards wide of its mark.

The black kid spun around, then started sprinting up the hill.

Jerome and his friends set off after him.

"Get goin', nigger!" Jerome shouted between breaths. He could hear Eddie panting next to him, struggling to pull a large rock out of his pocket while he was running.

A blue van passed the white kids and slowed down when it reached the black boy. Jerome saw a side door pop open . . . a white arm extended to hold it while the black kid clambered in. The van had the stenciled letters of a local television station on the side.

"Ah shit," Jerome slowed to a walk. "Some niggers got all the luck. I can't wait to get me one."

"Let's go, man, there's bound to be more at the school."

Jerome led the group at a half trot around the corner next to the school. He was still flushed and excited from his near miss with the black student.

"Damn!" As soon as they turned the corner, the group came smack up against a cordon of police stretched across the street. Feeling like a field marshal leading his troops, Jerome quickly scanned the other side streets. Each sported its own string of riot-equipped police.

"No way in," he announced to his friends.

"Aw, let's get back."

"Naw, let's wait just a minute and see what happens." Jerome was loath to give up the chase now. "Maybe we can pop one of the buses when it comes by."

"OK, pal, either get into school or move it." A police sergeant, holding his long wooden baton in both hands walked up to them.

"We ain't going to school as long as there's niggers in there," Jerome spoke for the group.

"Then get moving. On down the street away from here."

"This is still a public street, ain't it?" Jerome asked defiantly.

"Not today, pal, and not for you. Now move it or I'm going to haul your ass in."

Jerome was about to answer when he saw one yellow school bus pull up in front of the high school. He watched in exasperation as a handful of black students stepped off, looked around curiously, and walked into the school. The only people to greet them, besides police officers, were reporters and camera crews restricted to the monument grounds a hundred yards away.

Jerome pivoted angrily and stalked down the hill toward the project. He remembered the headlines last year when hundreds of whites camped out in front of South Boston High School and screamed at the buses when they drove up. By the time those buses left Southie, Jerome remembered with satisfaction, they looked like they'd been through World War III.

He felt humiliated. People in Charlestown didn't like busing, but they weren't going to turn out in angry numbers to block the buses the way it had happened in Southie. He'd boasted all summer about how they were going to show Southie, and here only he and a handful of friends were at the high school. The blacks walked peacefully into school right in front of them.

Back at the project, people were still angry at the helicopter that continued to patrol overhead and the helmeted policemen who now marched up and down Bunker Hill

Street in formation. Occasionally, ten or twelve motor-cycles roared by in a noisy group. People thought the police had overdone it.

"We ain't done *nothin'* to those buses, and look what they do to us!" a woman complained to her state repre-sentative, who nodded his head sympathetically. That's about all she would get out of him. In Southie, politicians were eager to lead anti-busing marches and boldly urged people to defy the court orders. In Charlestown, politi-cians were sympathetic, but they didn't want their futures tied so closely to the success or failure of the anti-busers.

Jerome noticed that the police with their high-powered rifles were gone now from the roofs. He smiled and hur-ried inside one of the buildings.

"Go through the trash and pick up as many bottles as you can," he whispered. "Meet me on the top, but keep down! Don't let nobody see you!"

Jerome felt a new rush of excitement. He felt the same sort of exhilaration he had known as a little kid when he'd gone to a war movie and came out feeling like the hero who had outwitted the enemy.

Crouched on the roof, Jerome saw Charlestown in a new way. The project looked seedier up here where you could see the expensive townhouses on the hill that young professional people had started to buy. There, the roof decks had little gardens and lawn chairs. Here there was just soot and broken glass. Jerome resented the people in the townhouses. Most of them weren't real Townies, they'd just moved in because the houses were nice and were cheap. Sometimes they complained they didn't feel accepted here. Jerome knew they never would be.

His friends huddled around him, their arms full of the trash-can booty.

"OK, everybody throw at the cops on the count of three. Then don't wait to see what happens. Everybody get out of here. When we get downstairs, we all split up. Meet you in the back later."

"One! Two! Three!"

Jerome hurled two large bottles as hard as he could. Seconds later he heard them crash on the pavement four stories below. He reached down for two more rocks and stood triumphantly on the roof as he let them fly.

The gang of kids raced down the stairs, aware of the commotion and frenzy outside. Jerome, in the lead, took three stairs at a time. Past the broken doors and obscene graffiti, past the urine-soaked corners.

When he hit bottom he didn't stop, but sped out the back door and sprinted toward the next building, a few dozen yards away. He could hear sirens wailing behind him and wondered if anyone had been hurt. Before he reached the building he heard the shouts of police behind him. He wasn't sure if they had seen him. He ducked into the building and held his breath, trying to decide whether to risk a peek. He did and it was enough to tell him he'd been spotted. He slammed the door shut and fled out the back.

As he dashed for a third refuge, he heard the smash of glass breaking in the street and the shouts of kids from above. Apparently he'd started something.

The smell of burning wood in the late-night air seemed out of place in early September. Jerome hardly noticed the trash-can fires glowing in the street as he squatted on the ground with two other boys. They were preoccupied with what they were doing, pausing only to exchange stories of the afternoon's heroics. The black students themselves had left Charlestown unmolested, but there had been more than one game of cat-and-mouse through the project with the police.

Jerome squinted through the cigarette smoke curling up from his lips as he concentrated on tying knots in the wire at his feet. He felt important and tough. Three boys had been arrested earlier in the day, but they were already back in the project, ready for the night.

"OK," Jerome announced, straightening. "Let's see what it looks like."

He wrapped a loop of wire around a telephone pole, then motioned to a group across the street. Soon a wire about four feet off the ground stretched taut across the street.

"That ought to take care of 'em." Jerome dusted his hands in satisfaction.

"What now?" one of the older Townies crossed the street and came up to Jerome. "What now?" Jerome recognized him as one of the men who hung out at the

Broadway Taven. He still wore his high school letter jacket, although he must have been out of school for at least ten years now. Jerome flipped his cigarette away with the smugness of a newly respected leader.

"Now we get 'em down here," he told the older man.

The two dozen men and boys milling around on Bunker Hill Street seemed to be waiting for a cue.

"Let's do it!"

The street exploded with the sounds of smashing glass and firecrackers. New fires leapt up in the street from matches set to gasoline-soaked rags. From the other side of Charlestown came the howl of sirens. Jerome thrilled with anticipation.

"OK, everybody back! Everybody back!" he ordered, herding the group several yards behind the almost invisible wire. Some of the men had to be grabbed by the shoulder and pushed down the street. Many of them had been drinking all day and seemed to forget the plan.

The white lights of a dozen police motorcycles cut through the darkened street and they roared toward the group of shouting men.

"You guys pissed about this afternoon?" Jerome screamed his taunt at the rapidly approaching headlights. "Come and get us!"

He jumped up and down in excitement as the motorcycles sped down the last block separating the Townies from the police.

The first cop to hit the wire gasped so loudly Jerome could hear him several yards away. The man flew to one side, his bike spinning out from under him. Jerome stomped his feet in glee and pounded Eddie on the back.

The second policeman realized what had happened only moments before he hit the wire himself. But it was too late. He caught the wire in the neck with such force that it snapped under his weight. He stayed on his motorcycle for a split second, then flipped out of control.

The street suddenly seemed filled with confusion: motorcycles circling, men running, shouts for an ambulance. A couple of the slower guys had been grabbed by the policemen, who hustled them into a police wagon.

Jerome already was backing away from the action, trying to take it all in at once. The two injured policemen were still sprawled on the ground as their colleagues shouted angrily at the night and pulled at the twisted wire. Jerome kicked over a burning trash can in satisfaction, sending a geyser of sparks into the night air. He anticipated night after night of skirmishes with the police. He danced backward happily toward the dark safety of the project.

Officer McMaster

"YOU GONNA RUN DOWN your grandmother today, McMaster?"

The woman, her hair rolled into fat pink curlers, screeched out the front door at the passing motorcycle. Officer Ashton McMaster heard the taunt, but his face remained impassive. He had more pressing business on his mind. Just moments ago, his radio had squawked urgently: a group of kids was gathering along the bus route at the bottom of the hill. The buses of black students from South Boston High would have to pass right by them.

"Here we go again," he thought to himself.

He pushed the thin accelerator down hard as he rounded G street, then slowed when he saw another motorcycle policeman, Eric Stevens, idling on the corner.

"We got trouble?" he pulled alongside Stevens.

"Not really. Bunch of kids in front of the project." He pointed several blocks away. "Soon as we get more help we'll move 'em along."

They waited in silence, watching the afternoon sun sparkle on the bay a few blocks away. School was only a few days old, and already there was much more trouble than anyone had expected.

"I hate this." McMaster broke the silence suddenly. "I really hate this."

Stevens grunted.

"I used to live here, you know."

"Here in Southie?"

"Yeah. Brought up here. Just moved out to Dedham a few years ago. Thought my folks would have a fit. They still live up near the high school."

It seemed like a long time ago. High school, then the Marines, then the police academy. Now marriage and two kids and a small house in the suburbs.

"Yeah. Never thought I'd be coming back to Southie like this," McMaster mused, taking off his blue helmet and looking around.

"I probably know a lot of those kids." He pointed toward the crowd of youths milling in front of the housing project. "Their older brothers or sisters anyway."

"You're gonna hate crackin' their heads, then."

"Nah. They're good kids. They'll move along. They don't mean nothin'." The roar of several approaching motorcycles cut him off. A captain was in the lead.

"All right. We're just gonna ask them to move along. No rough stuff unless we have trouble. They're holding up the buses at the high school until we get these kids away from the street."

McMaster was on his bike and halfway to the project when he heard his name.

"Ash! Hey, Ash!" A blond-haired boy about sixteen broke away from a group standing on the corner. McMaster slowed his bike, then stopped.

"Hey, Maxie. How ya doin'?" He was surprised he remembered the boy's name. He and Maxie's older brother had been close friends in high school, but that was a decade ago. He had only run into Maxie or his brother off and on since then.

"Good. Real good. You're a cop now, huh?"

"How'd you guess?" McMaster laughed. He saw the other motorcycle police up ahead, moving slowly through the crowd, telling people to get back on the sidewalk. Some did.

"How come they got you back here protectin' the niggers?"

"No choice, Maxie. You go where they tell you."

"Yeah. Makes a lot of people mad, the cops protectin' the niggers like that."

"I know." McMaster remembered the woman yelling at him an hour ago. He kicked his bike into gear. "See ya." He spotted Stevens on the next street corner, waving his arms as he talked to a group of kids.

"What do they gotta come to our schools for?" One of the boys spit angrily.

"I'm not gonna get into a debate with you. Just get movin'."

McMaster stayed back, unsure of whether to intervene or not. Finally the group dispersed, some wandering toward Carson Beach, the others back to the housing project.

"I never get into an argument with them," Stevens said as he watched them go. "Just gets them riled up."

"What happened to the buses?"

"Finally took them the long way around. Afraid of the crowd here."

Stevens leaned his large frame back in the seat and rubbed the nape of his neck. "So. You're a Southie kid, McMaster. What do you think of all this?"

"I think it's a damn shame."

"How come?"

"Look, you live in Southie and the high school is everything. When you're a little kid, you look forward to goin' there. The football stars are heroes. Everybody goes to the games whether they got kids playin' or not. There's a lot of spirit here.

"See all those old guys walkin' around, still wearing their Southie high school jackets?" he continued. "That's because it's still important here. Then you bring in a lot of outsiders and tell people they've got to send their kids to Roxbury and what happens? The whole thing's ruined."

"But the kids in Roxbury got lousy schools."

"So Southie kids should share the lousy schools?"

"No, I mean don't the black kids deserve a good place, too?"

"Sure they do. But why don't they just fix up the schools in Roxbury? If they spent all the money on that

that they're spending on busing, Roxbury High would be like Harvard."

"Too late for that now, pal."

"Yeah, well, I'll bet the black kids don't like it any better than the white kids."

"You headin' back?"

"In a minute. I'm gonna stop over at Whitney's and see my old man." Since his retirement two years ago, McMaster's father spent most afternoon's in Whitney's, a small bar with a regular clientele of neighborhood men. McMaster had had his first legal beer there.

Whitney's was small and dark. A few old pinball machines leaned against one wall, a cigarette machine against another. The place was only half filled now. It would be busier after work. McMaster waved at the regulars, men he'd known all his life, and found his father at his usual stool at the end of the bar.

"Hey! Ashton! What a surprise! What are you doin' here?"

"Busing. I got assigned to the high school."

"Oh. Well, let me buy you a beer."

"Sorry. Not 'til I get into civilian clothes."

"Oh, yeah. I thought they had you workin' out in Dorchester." He followed his son's career closely. Being a policeman was highly regarded in Southie, where unemployment was high and many who did work could find only unskilled jobs.

"I was. Then all the trouble with busing here and we all got assigned to the high school."

A newcomer about his father's age joined them. "Saw you out in front of the project a while ago. Didn't push any of those kids around, did you?"

"Didn't have to."

"I should hope not" — the man thrust his face closer to McMaster's — "since they're only standin' up for all of us and our way of life."

"Yeah." McMaster tried to be as noncommittal as possible.

"But you wouldn't bust them anyway, would you, since you're from Southie?"

"If they were breakin' the law I'd have to."

"But what if they were just trying to keep those coloreds away? You don't believe in busing, do you?"

"Not at all," he said truthfully.

"Then what are you gonna do when your commanding officer tells you to bust some dame's head, and she's your old Sunday school teacher?"

"It won't come to that."

"Hrmmph," the man snorted. "Dreamer."

The police radio on McMaster's belt crackled to life. "All officers report to the Old Colony Housing Project at once."

"See ya." He ran out the door and jumped onto his motorcycle. The project was just around the corner. He pulled up short when he saw nearly two hundred people — men, women, and teenagers — lining the sidewalks and spilling into the street. Officer Stevens joined him.

"I thought this was all over," McMaster said.

"Turns out they still got three buses of blacks at the elementary school."

"Here comes help." Several police cars and wagons and buses arrived almost simultaneously, each one carrying a load of police in riot gear. McMaster was surprised to see the superintendent of police in charge himself.

"All right. You guys line up here." He waved the police still pouring out of the buses onto one side of the street. "You guys," he yelled to McMaster and several motorcycle police, "Take the other side. Keep 'em back."

McMaster pulled down the visor on his helmet. He slipped his bike into first gear and started slowly down the street. He thought the crowd seemed more restless and curious than angry.

"OK, folks. Back up on the sidewalk." Most stepped back on the curb as he passed. Some even called out his name. Word had gotten around that McMaster was a Southie boy.

McMaster quickly realized that as soon as he was a few yards away, most of the people who had stepped up on the curb were back in the street again.

"McMaster! What are you doin'?" It was the captain. "I told you to move 'em back! Stevens! Bradley! Get over there and help him."

"Hey, Ash! How's your Dad doin'?" It was a woman who lived down the street from his parents.

"Mrs. Leland. You shouldn't be out here. There might be trouble."

"Just had to see what was happening. So how's your Dad enjoying retirement?"

McMaster was aware that it wasn't the time or place for a friendly chat. People were wandering into the street all around him. He hoped the captain was busy elsewhere.

"Guess it agrees with him, Mrs. Leland."

"That's good. The man deserves to take it easy. You stop down to see us next time you visit, hear?" She spotted another neighbor and was gone.

A bullhorn blasted the air. "All right, folks. Everybody move back on the sidewalk. I know you all want to see what's goin' on, but nothing's goin' on. Nothing to get excited about today." McMaster was relieved when the crowd took a few steps back. They seemed as interested in the police as they did in the school buses that would soon pass by.

The voice on the bullhorn was angry now. "I'm gonna give you folks thirty seconds to clear this street, then we're gonna have to start pushin'."

McMaster's stomach clenched. He knew what that meant. He and the other motorcycle police would ride into the crowd, breaking it into knots and forcing people back. He looked around. Several faces in the crowd smiled at him.

"Hey, Ash!" McMaster spun sharply. It was Maxie again. Right in the middle of the street.

"Maxie! Get outa here! Didn't you hear him?"

"Come on, man, I just wanna see those niggers go by. I ain't gonna hurt 'em." Maxie was grinning, his young face flushed with excitement. McMaster spotted a brick, half hidden behind his back.

"I just wanna get close and give those little bastards the finger."

"Move 'em back!" The bullhorn shrieked.

"Move, Maxie," McMaster hissed at him, "move on back!"

"Come on, Ash," Maxie laughed, "I know you're with us!"

"Move 'em back!"

McMaster clenched his teeth and started easing his bike forward, straight toward Maxie. He hoped the boy would realize he meant business and get off the street. But Maxie, still smiling to himself, turned to stare up the street toward the elementary school.

McMaster looked around nervously. All around him police were nudging people toward the sidewalk. The other side of the street was already cleared, police standing in a line in front of the crowd, nightsticks in hand. Down the street he saw two policemen haul off a woman in a Nazi helmet.

"Crazy lady," he muttered. She showed up at most demonstrations and usually got arrested.

"McMaster! Move that kid or arrest him!"

McMaster got slowly off his bike. "Come on, Maxie, let's go."

Maxie looked at him in amazement. "You gonna arrest me, Ash?"

"Move your butt outa here and I won't have to," Mc-Master hissed.

It was too late. The superintendent himself strode over with two other policemen.

"What the hell is goin' on here?" He grabbed Maxie roughly by the arm and knocked the brick out of his hand. "McMaster, call for a wagon."

"He wasn't doin' nothin'," a woman on the sidewalk yelled.

"Yeah. Let 'im go!"

The four officers pulled closer together, Maxie still in the grip of the superintendent.

"Hey, Ash! Come on, man! Let him go!"

McMaster grunted as he felt a sharp tug on his arm. He yanked it back automatically before he realized a man had broken away from the crowd and was trying to push by him to reach Maxie.

"Let's get him!" The crowd converged on them from all sides. McMaster was terrified. Moments ago he felt in control. Now he felt outnumbered. He jabbed with his elbows and kept his head down.

In front of him, he could see the superintendent, still clutching Maxie with one muscular arm, swinging his nightstick with the other. Hands grabbed at them from everywhere. What was only a few moments seemed like hours.

McMaster realized other police were around them now, he could hear them grunting and shouting as they pushed against the mob. A moment later it was all over.

McMaster and the superintendent stood panting, looking around warily to make sure the assault was really over. Maxie still struggled weakly between them.

"OK, punk, here we go." The superintendent turned as the police wagon backed up to them. Two policemen jumped out and opened the double doors in the rear. Inside, McMaster could see two thin wooden benches on each side of the van. There were no windows.

Maxie's eyes widened. "No! No!" The crowd hissed.

McMaster pushed up close to the superintendent. "We don't really have to do this, sir." He whispered urgently. "The kid didn't really do anything."

"Are you kiddin' me?" the superintendent asked. His sleeve was ripped and his face had thin streaks of blood. "He was standin' in the middle of the street with a brick in his hand." He pushed Maxie forward roughly. "In you go, kid. You ride with him, McMaster."

McMaster climbed in behind Maxie, thankful to escape the angry crowd. When the doors slammed shut, it was dark and close inside. He heard the steel bar drop across the latch. Through slats against the back wall, he caught glimpses of the scene. He could hear better than he could see.

"You pig, McMaster, you nigger-lovin' pig!"

"Don't come back to Southie, creep!"

McMaster turned to Maxie, huddled in a corner of the van.

"Look, Maxie, when we get you out, you've gotta explain to those people that I didn't want this to happen."

"You never should've took this job if you didn't want this to happen."

"What was I gonna do?"

"You never shoulda been here helpin' the niggers take over our school."

"You go where they tell you to go. I told you that."

McMaster could feel the wagon picking up speed. "Hey, you know I'm not for busing. I'm just doin' my job."

"Your job stinks."

McMaster gave up. He looked out the tiny back window and watched the streets of Southie disappear behind him.

Linda

THE VISITOR sat in Ted's coffee shop and stirred her coffee idly, gazing out the window in front of her. Cleary Square was full of lazy business this October afternoon. Housewives strolled past the shops, a few pushing baby carriages. Businessmen, their hands stuffed into their pockets, stood in pairs here and there on the sidewalk, talking. Each street corner seemed to boast its own contingent of high school students leaning against the lampposts, keeping a casual eye out for passing cars that might contain friends.

Cleary Square had long been the heart of Hyde Park, a huge Boston neighborhood sprawled across the city's southern border. Hyde Park didn't enjoy the intimacy of some older neighborhoods closer to the city's core, like South Boston or East Boston, even though many of Hyde Park's residents originally were from there.

Moving to Hyde Park was usually counted as a move up the social ladder. The houses were nicer than in the old neighborhood and most of them had yards. Nearly everyone owned a car. Many of the people who moved to Hyde Park brought their opinions with them. Although black families lived here and there in the community, many people wanted Hyde Park to stay mostly white, the way it had always been. If they didn't have the rough-and-tumble attitude their cousins in Charlestown had toward busing — they would have balked at stoning buses — some were just as determined to resist it in other ways.

The visitor was just about to order another cup of coffee when she noticed a red Ford pull up in front and double-park while a balding man in a checked sports coat jumped out. He hurried into the coffee shop and looked quizzically around.

"Mr. Holmes?" the visitor asked.

"Oh, hi." He came over and stood by the small table. "Sorry to be late. You ready to go? I'll drive you back here later."

"Now," he said, settling behind the wheel. "We're trusting you to forget how you got here, OK? Anybody asks you, you just don't remember. We never let reporters in, and we're just making an exception this once."

The bustle of Cleary Square gave way to the quiet of residential streets lined with gracious homes. Although most of the older parts of the city were jammed with three-deckers, this corner of Hyde Park sported rambling ranch-style homes with spacious lawns. It could have been mistaken for any suburb in the state.

They turned off the main street onto a quiet drive that ended in a circle. The driveway of one of the houses was jammed with cars. They pulled in behind them, the rear end of the Ford hanging out into the street.

"Don't even look at the house number," Holmes advised. "That way you don't have to forget it later."

They entered the back door without knocking and hurried down the stairs to the basement. Once there, the visitor could hear a murmur of voices.

Holmes pushed open a door, and they stepped into a large room that obviously had once been a playroom; its boxes of toys and bikes were now stuffed into corners. About fifteen students sat around three long tables, scribbling in notebooks while a gray-haired woman standing at the front of the room pointed at a map, tracing European countries.

They had entered one of the so-called alternative schools that had sprung up around Boston in strictest secrecy. The classes met clandestinely in basements like this one, and students were reminded each day they mustn't tell anyone where they went to school. The school was not certified by the city, and because everyone under sixteen was required by law to attend a licensed school, these schools were illegal.

If they were discovered, the adults who had set the school up and the parents who enrolled their children could be subject to arrest for keeping children out of school and trying to subvert the court desegregation order. They didn't care, though. They would rather have their kids go to an illegal private school than be bused to a legal public one — plus, this alternative school was all white.

Linda frowned in concentration at the page in front of her, but glanced surreptitiously at the visitor from time to time out of the corner of her eye. She had been warned that a reporter would be coming today, but Linda didn't know if anyone would be asked any questions.

Linda would have been a junior at Hyde Park High School if she had gone to public school this year. She wouldn't have had to ride a bus; in fact, she lived so close that she could have walked every day the way she had last year. But her parents vehemently opposed the desegregation order and refused to let her or her three younger brothers have anything to do with public schools.

Linda was going to the alternative school. So far her brothers were just staying at home. The parochial schools were so crowded they couldn't get in there.

Linda's father had helped set up the alternative school with ten other parents he had known from various anti-busing groups. It cost fifteen dollars a week per student, which was just enough to pay the teacher and buy some books.

Linda thought going to school in someone's basement was a lot different from going to Hyde Park High. They had the same teacher for every subject and didn't go to a cafeteria or homeroom, of course. Since there was only one teacher, the school day was shorter. Linda left home at eight and was usually home by one. She was a little worried she might be missing something, but her father was happy because the alternative school, he said, stressed the "fundamentals." He meant it spurned modern math and novels like *Catcher in the Rye* and stressed the "three Rs."

The reporter whispered to Holmes, who looked blankly ahead for a minute, then nodded slightly. The reporter could interview one of the kids if no names were used. He pointed to Linda. He knew it would make her father happy.

They sat together at one of the long tables after everyone else had left. Linda tugged at her long hair. She was excited about being interviewed, but she was nervous, too. Her father was always swearing about the "liberal media," which, he said, never told the awful stories about things that really happened in the schools after they desegregated. She was surprised Mr. Holmes had left them alone, but relieved, too.

"Do you enjoy going to school here?"

"Oh, yes. All the kids are real nice and the teacher is good, too. She used to teach in Boston, you know, but hasn't been able to get a part-time job this year so she came to work for us."

"Why are you going here?"

"Because of the busing. My parents didn't want me to go to bad schools in bad neighborhoods. You can't dictate where people have to go to school in a free country."

It was a theme the reporter had heard from the speakers' platforms at countless anti-busing rallies. She wondered how many Linda had attended.

"Do you miss anything from your old school?"

"Oh, no," answered Linda promptly. "We have books that are just as good; a lot of them are newer than we had at Hyde Park High."

Linda was sitting up straight now and looking the reporter right in the eye. She seemed pleased with herself, as if she were giving the right answers in class.

"But don't you miss other things?" The reporter gestured at the room around her.

"Oh, no," Linda said confidently, then paused. "Like what?"

"Oh, football games and field trips and pep rallies." The reporter searched her memory, trying to recall what high school students did when they weren't in class. "You know, going to the prom and decorating the gym for the homecoming dance. Didn't you used to do things like that at Hyde Park High?"

"Yes," Linda admitted grudgingly, "but we'll do all that stuff here too as soon as we get enough money to open the academy. It'll be just like a regular school."

"But you won't even be here then," the reporter pointed out. "It will be years before you can even find a suitable building and get it equipped."

Linda pursed her lips and stared sullenly in front of her. The reporter shifted ground suddenly. She hadn't realized Linda thought a new school would be operating soon.

"Who can go to school here?"

"Anyone is eligible." Linda relaxed, feeling she was back on safe territory. "We would accept anyone who is qualified, regardless of race, creed, or color." She sounded as if she had rehearsed the answer.

"How about a black student?"

"Sure, they could go to school here," Linda said. "Of course, none have ever applied," she added a bit smugly.

The afternoon sun cut a patch of yellow on the linoleum floor. The reporter was anxious to wrap up the interview, but she was also curious about this girl who seemed to have such a combination of pat responses and misinformation.

"Why don't you want to go to college?" the reporter asked suddenly.

Linda's eyes blinked wide in surprise.

"But I am going to college," she said, for once without pretense. "Probably to U. Mass., where my sister went."

"Where are you going to go for high school then?"

"I'm going *here* for high school."

The reporter shook her head sadly. "You see," she said gently, "this school doesn't count. It's an illegal school because it isn't certified. You can't go to college unless you have a high school certificate, and this school" — she waved vaguely at the basement — "just isn't considered a school."

Linda laughed. "No, no, you're all wrong. My parents know I want to go to college, and they'd never let me go to a high school that didn't count." She started collecting her books and notebooks, talking faster now, the talk punctuated by nervous laughter.

"No, no. I'm going to college in two years. We'll have the academy real soon and I'll go there for one year and then to college. I'm going to college and be a teacher probably. I don't know. It'll be fun." She was putting on her coat.

"I have to go now." She reached for the door handle. "I have some homework to do and stuff."

The reporter snapped her notebook shut and stood up. She heard the oil burner click on on the other side of the wall, probably in a laundry room. She looked around. Without a teacher or student or books, the room no longer pretended to be anything other than a basement that was masquerading, briefly, as something else.

Helen

HELEN BARRETT winced as the elevated train clattered by overhead. She clutched the steering wheel and hunched her shoulders involuntarily, waiting for the rush of metal striking metal to subside. Although she had driven this route for nearly three years now, Helen could never get used to the unexpected roar of the subway that ran on tracks built up over the street.

"Sometimes I feel guilty putting you through this," said Dave, sitting next to her.

Helen negotiated the car around several double-parked cars.

"I don't mind, really. I enjoy the company." For several months Helen and Dave had been a car pool ("I'm the car and he's the pool," she often put it, laughingly). They both worked at Faulkner Hospital, she as a nurse, he as a respiratory technician. She had once offered to drop him off at the subway on her way home, and it had soon become a habit whenever their shifts coincided. They would meet in the parking lot and drive the few miles to Egleston Square, where Dave would catch the subway downtown while Helen continued home to Dorchester and her family.

Helen always refused to take any money, even though it was a detour for her. But Dave insisted on taking her to lunch every few weeks and one day showed up with a box of saltwater taffy for her kids.

"They need it more than I do," Helen had smiled as she patted her ample stomach. She used to tease Dave, who was just out of college, that if he didn't put some meat on *his* bones he'd never catch any of the athletic-looking young women at the hospital. Dave told her not to worry. They liked teasing back and forth on their rides to Egleston station, even though they didn't really know each other very well.

They waited at a stoplight, Helen resting her hands on the steering wheel, Dave drumming his fingers to a tune on the radio.

"I know what it is!" Helen said suddenly.

Dave started. "What what is?"

"It's spring! That's what's different about tonight! I thought I just felt good because it's Friday. But it's because spring is here. At last!"

She looked appreciatively at the shaft of sunlight catching the tip of a three-decker home nearby. Just a few weeks ago, it seemed, they had driven home in the dark. Now it was only dusk. Even the peeling gray tracks of the elevated looked nicer in the fading light.

"Doesn't take much to make you happy." But Dave seemed pleased, too.

"Don't bother driving me all the way to Egleston tonight," he suggested. "You get home to your kids. I can hoof it from here." He looked out the window. Just a few blocks back, they had been driving through streets lined with neat white homes with black shiny shutters. The old houses were big and comfortable looking. A few minutes' ride, however, had brought them to this tattered, rundown neighborhood. Both of the neighborhoods were integrated, but the first one had more white people and the second one had more blacks.

"You're not going to walk," Helen said adamantly. "See that group? Think I want you walking by them?" Nearly a dozen black teenage boys lounged on the street corner, a few smoking, a few drinking beer. She remembered hearing over the last few days reports of blacks being beaten up in Southie and Dorchester, at subway stations and on buses. Whenever that happened, it seemed like a chain reaction began that carried into the black neighborhoods. And although the incidents of violence against whites were not a frequent occurrence, when they did happen, they were brutal. Helen stepped on the gas.

"It's not like we're the only white people around here," Dave pointed out.

"No, it's not," Helen replied, "but those kids would love to snitch a nice young man's wallet — white or black."

She cruised up Washington Street and pulled expertly up to the curb.

"Here you go, boss."

"Thanks, Helen. See you tomorrow."

Helen sat a moment, watching Dave's brown jacket disappear up the steps, hoping he wouldn't have to wait too long for a train. She eased the car into first and looked over her shoulder at the oncoming traffic. The day's burst of springtime had faded already in the dusk, and she snapped her headlights on.

She was just turning back to the steering wheel when she saw them. Several young black men, perhaps the group she and Dave had seen on the corner, were now standing idly next to her car. They didn't seem to be paying any special attention to her, but they didn't move on either. Suddenly, Helen felt nervous.

She glanced over her shoulder again at the stream of traffic, hoping for a break that would allow her to pull away from the curb. A car had parked in front of her and she had to tug at the wheel to maneuver her car clear of it. She heard a laugh from the group on the sidewalk and pulled harder at the wheel, too anxious now even to look at them.

She felt herself panicking as she remembered the white man who had been caught at a traffic light in Roxbury a few weeks ago. He had done nothing, and a group of black youths had dragged him from his car and beaten him until he was unconscious. He was still in a coma, and the papers said that if he came out of it, he would be a vegetable for the rest of his life.

"Hey, you white Momma . . . !" Helen looked at the boys now leering over the front of the car. She knew she was in trouble.

Helen felt weak, but she swung wildly into action as the realization hit her that they might try to enter the car. She began punching down the locks on the doors. With a sob, she reached for the lock on the passenger's side, where only a minute before, Dave had sat joking with her. She was too late.

"What's a matter, Momma? Getting scared?" A kid had opened the door on the passenger's side and now had his face just inches from Helen's. She could smell the liquor on his breath as he glared at her. She turned her head away and made a last desperate tug at the wheel.

With one quick move, her intruder turned the keys in the ignition, pulled them out, and threw them on the ground in back of him.

"Now, Momma, us kids here owe you somethin'."

Helen began screaming hysterically. The boy, who seemed too young to be so mean, returned her screams with obscene shouts. He backed out of the car.

Suddenly, the front seat exploded in glass. A rock pounded off the windshield, leaving a web of splintered glass behind.

"Oh, my God!" Helen sobbed just as a second rock sailed through the side window, shattering it, and throwing pieces of glass into the side of her head. She screamed in pain, feeling the blood running through her mouth.

She tried to slide down in the seat, trying to get her large body around the steering wheel. She thought that if she could only get on the floor she could save herself. But as she tried to force her way down, a brick came through the windshield with such force it caught her in the chest and threw her back against the seat.

Helen could hear the shouts of excitement outside. The shouts grew louder with each rock, each brick. The group of young blacks continued to scream at her. She thought how much they hated her, and they didn't even know her. She heard a large object bounce off the hood, then into the windshield. There wasn't much left of the windshield.

Another brick came in the window on the passenger side. She put her arms around her head and was able to protect herself. But then another rock came in the open space that was the driver's window. It caught her on the head, then fell on her shoulder. She huddled over the steering wheel. Her nurse's training began to make her think: concussion, skull fracture. Then she heard her back window hit with a barrage of rocks. For one horrible moment, she wondered desperately if she would ever get out.

The blinking blue lights seemed to fill the air around her. She could hear sirens; they seemed so far away, yet she knew they were right next to her.

"Lady, lady, can you hear me?" Helen saw out of the corner of her eye a blue uniform, but she was getting dizzy and couldn't focus well.

"Jesus, they really got you, didn't they?"

Helen didn't answer, and willingly let herself slide into unconsciousness.

*   *   *

The recovery room at the Faulkner was oddly foreign, and it took Helen several minutes to figure out why, since she had worked at the Faulkner a dozen years, often ministering to patients in this very room. Suddenly she realized what it was: she had never before seen it from the patient's point of view.

She could count six beds besides her own in the long, narrow room. Each bed was separated from the next only by a curtain that was left pulled back except when a doctor or nurse was examining the patient. Helen wished she could have more privacy.

Her whole head pulsed rhythmically in pain. Gingerly she explored her injuries. Her left eye was puffy and nearly swollen shut. She could easily imagine how discolored it must be—all black and blue. Her tongue probed a tooth that wiggled when it was touched. She felt like crying. She had always prided herself on her perfect teeth. She hated to think of losing one.

Her hand crept cautiously up her forehead until she felt a wad of gauze, then a bandage, then more and more bandage — her head was encircled by a thick, tight ribbon of bandages. The blows to her head must have been worse than she realized. She remembered the nurse in the emergency room telling her, through her drugged fog, that she had had more than thirty stitches in her scalp, and they were waiting for X-ray results. If the stitches were in the left side of her head, where it was most tender, they must have shaved much of her hair. She was close to sobbing out loud when someone spoke her name.

"Mrs. Barrett? I'm Officer Connolly. I'm sorry to bother you, but you weren't in any shape to talk before. From the looks of our information, this was an unprovoked attack." Helen looked at the young, blond officer, twisting his cap in his hand.

"We want to catch the kids who did it. They all scattered as soon as they saw the cruiser coming, so we really need your cooperation."

Helen looked at him, still dazed, and still slightly drugged. She tried to speak, but her throat was too dry. She swallowed and asked in a whisper, "Why? Why did they do it?"

The officer handed her a plastic cup with a straw in it. He held it for her as she sipped some water.

"I don't know, ma'am. We've never had a year like this one," he said quietly, almost matching the softness in her voice. "Since this busing, it's been black against white," he paused, "and, I guess, white against black."

Helen looked at him quizzically. She tried to take a deep breath but was hit by pains. She remembered the brick. She shook her head.

"Sure, we had trouble before in some of the neighborhoods. You know, kids would open car doors and steal purses, things like that." He put his cap down on the small table next to her bed. "But this type of beating, no. White beats on black, then black beats on white, and then it starts all over again."

"Well, why don't they go after the people who beat up

the others?" Helen croaked, feeling herself filling up with tears. "Ohhh . . ." She turned away from the officer.

"Ma'am, I'm sorry, but we need your help. Can you give me any description of your assailants?"

Helen shut her eyes, trying to recollect. There had been that first black face only inches from hers. Surely she could remember him. But all she could come up with was the image of a sneering young face.

"All I can tell you is he was young and black."

"Who was?"

"The one who came into the car, threw out the keys. He was young."

"How about the others?"

"How many were there?"

"Witnesses put it at fifteen."

"Oh, my lord." Helen imagined the scene. Fifteen teen-agers ringing her small car, pelting it with rocks and bricks, shouting and laughing. She felt weak again.

"But if there were witnesses, why didn't anyone help?"

"Because it happened so fast. It was over in less than a minute. And anyway, these kids were mean."

Helen thought, No kidding. She felt herself starting to get angry.

"Did you get any of them?"

"No, ma'am, a patrol car was just on a normal run when they came across the incident. There were only two officers and they went to your aid first."

Helen didn't say anything.

The officer picked up his cap and said, somewhat defensively, "It's very hard. It was dark and they split as soon as they saw the police. If we don't have accurate descriptions, well, I'm not too hopeful." He turned to leave.

"But, Mrs. Barrett, you should feel lucky. Remember what they did to that white guy in Roxbury a few weeks ago. He's a goner. Make sure you stay out of those neighborhoods. God knows, I'd never let my wife drive through them."

Helen watched the officer leave and mumbled to herself, "Who would have known? I've never been afraid to go anyplace in this city. I've never had any trouble. And neither have the kids. They go to school with black kids. . . ."

"There you are!" A familiar tone broke her train of thought.

"Dave . . ."

"God, I feel awful about this. I can't believe I didn't wait until you were gone. There was a train coming. I didn't hear anything. I just never thought . . ." He stood over her hesitantly.

"Not your fault, Dave. Not anybody's fault. I'll be just fine."

"We should have known . . . with all the trouble and all."

"Dave, I've been driving through Egleston Square for most of my life! I just can't believe it really happened."

Helen shuddered involuntarily.

"Oh, your husband was here. He spent most of the night here, but had to leave to get the kids off. He seems like a nice guy."

Helen thought briefly how nice it was that Dave got to meet a member of her family. Then her mind jolted back to what Dave had said.

"I've been out all night? Oh, Lord, Tom and the children must be so upset, so worried."

"No, they're OK. Your husband talked to the kids a lot. We knew you were going to be OK." Dave smiled. "I'll leave you alone now. But I'll be back on my break to check in."

Helen sank back in her pillows. She closed her eyes and tried to escape into sleep. She could sense someone approaching her bed and moving around her. A hand lifted the bandage on her head a bit and she opened her eyes a crack.

She stifled a scream. A broad black face was only inches from hers. It was a moment before she realized he was wearing hospital whites.

"Sorry to wake you up. I just need to check this. I'm Mark, a student nurse. Call me if you need anything. I should change your sheet while I'm here, though."

Helen recoiled involuntarily as Mark grasped her arm. He looked up.

"I'm not going to hurt you, Mrs. Barrett," he said softly.

"Sorry." But Helen could not take her eyes off his hand, so black against the white skin of her arm. She clenched her teeth during the sheet-changing routine. "I've never had anything against black people," she muttered to herself over and over. "I've never had anything against black people."

The scenes from her car kept replaying in her head. She watched the top of Mark's head and had to restrain herself from shouting at him, asking him why they had attacked her when she had never done anything to them.

His head came close to hers again and she shrank back, not realizing at first that he was merely fluffing the pillow. She watched his every motion wordlessly as he moved around the bed, not realizing until he was gone that she had been grinding her teeth together the whole time.

She lay back again and tried to relax, tried to bring her feelings into line.

She began to cry.

Larry

LARRY HOWE shifted silently on the hard wooden bench. In front of him, beyond the polished banister that separated spectators from the rest of the courtroom, beyond the battery of lawyers sitting at long mahogany tables in the middle of the room, the judge was speaking.

Larry shuffled his feet. He tried to pay attention, but he was bored.

"Sit still!" his mother hissed. She leaned forward intently. Like the other Boston Latin School parents in court today, she hung on every word. The fate of the school might be discussed today and she wanted to be certain the Latin parents would get their say. She had insisted that Larry come along because, she said, it would be a good experience.

Larry's mind wandered again. Outside the courtroom it looked like a nice spring day. He wished he were outside. Suddenly everyone around him started standing up and putting on their jackets.

"I miss something?" he asked his mother.

"He's not going to decide today. It doesn't sound good, though. He said the question was whether or not Latin should be treated like other schools. And that's the whole point! Latin's not like other schools! And we want to keep it that way!"

Nearly everyone thought Boston Latin was the best school in the city. Its curriculum was superior and nearly all of its graduates went to college. Latin alumni liked to boast that it was the oldest public school in the country, founded in 1635, one year before Harvard University. Over the years the path from Latin to Harvard became well beaten.

Latin didn't accept just anyone. Each year, thousands of students took the SSAT test. Latin admitted only the couple hundred who scored highest. When he took the test, Larry hadn't had much trouble. His mother had been grooming him for it for years.

"So what do you think the judge is gonna do?" He stood next to his mother as she waited for one of the lawyers to join her.

"I couldn't begin to predict what he's going to do. What I'm *afraid* he is going to do is lower the admissions standards so more blacks can get in. At least that's what he's talking about."

"Oh." Larry didn't really care one way or the other, but he knew his mother did.

"He says Latin should be just as integrated as every other school." As it was, Boston Latin was overwhelmingly white. For the first two years of desegregation, the judge had left it alone. Now he wondered whether more blacks should be able to attend the city's best high school. But that meant changing the test or doing away with it altogether, something Larry's mother fiercely opposed.

"You start letting in kids who aren't up to standards, just because they're black, and the whole school is going to suffer."

Larry had heard it many times before. But he knew she was off and running. "What's your class going to be like if all of a sudden there are a bunch of kids who can't keep up?" She answered her own question, "They're going to hold you all back, that's what. The good thing about a test is that it's totally fair. Black or white, you score high enough and you'll get in."

"I'm gonna wait out in the hall for you, OK?"

"I'll be along in a minute."

"Hey, Larry! What are you doin' here?" Larry was surprised to see Michael Wright walking out of the courtroom. They were both going to be seniors at Latin.

"Came with my mother. Who dragged you here?"

"Nobody," Michael smiled. "The state board of education picks a student representative every year, and I want to get it this year. I thought it would look good if I showed up here some." Larry smiled to himself. Everybody said that Mike Wright just had to grow a little and he'd be a perfect Boston politician. He was secretary of their class this year and already he was planning his campaign for vice president next year. In his sport jacket and tie he looked older than Larry, who hadn't bothered to change from his faded jeans and sneakers to come to court.

"So what do you think they're going to do to Latin?"

"Nothing, I expect. If they lower the admissions standards to let more blacks in, they'll ruin the school's reputation. And once it becomes like every other school in Boston, a lot of white parents are going to pull their kids out. I know my folks would send me to private school or something if there wasn't any Boston Latin."

"Mine probably would too. They think it's the only school in Boston that's worth anything."

"See?" Michael seemed very sure of himself, which made Larry uncomfortable. He surprised himself by picking an argument.

"I suppose it isn't fair to say every school in the city has to be integrated except Boston Latin, though."

"Come on." Michael was annoyed. "You want to drive all the whites from the city? I'm not saying blacks shouldn't go to Latin," he added hastily, "I'm just saying they have to pass the same test we had to pass. Otherwise they'll drag the whole place down. Unfair to us and unfair to them because they couldn't do the work."

Larry remembered Michael was on the debating team, still he hated to let it drop. "How can you expect them to do well on the test when they went to rotten elementary schools?"

"Hey! We went to elementary school in Boston, too."

"Yeah, but the ones in Roxbury are really sorry places."

"So fix them up. We shouldn't have to suffer for it."

Larry spotted his mother coming out of the courtroom. "Anything happen?"

"Nothing. Let's hope no news is good news."

One morning nearly two weeks later she discovered it wasn't. A phone call from a lawyer for one of the parents' organizations told her the federal judge wanted Boston Latin integrated. Thirty-five percent of the seats at Latin would be reserved for minority students — blacks and Hispanics. The admissions process itself would be altered, too. Grades and the test scores would both be considered. The only condition was that no one would be accepted to Latin, black or white, who did not score above the fiftieth percentile on the annual test. It was small comfort to Virginia Howe.

"You mean to tell me," she said angrily into the phone, "that a white boy who scores 70 on the test might not get in and a black boy who scores 55 will? That's not fair!"

"It could happen," the lawyer said soothingly, "but the court seems to feel the only way to integrate Latin is to hold some seats for minority kids."

"How about the academic standards at Latin when these kids can't do the work?"

"I don't know."

She hung up in disgust and looked at Larry, who was sitting on the couch reading.

"I'm only thankful that next year is your last year," she said. "Otherwise, I think we'd just have to move."

Larry looked around their spacious living room and

wondered if she really meant it. The family had moved to West Roxbury from another Boston neighborhood several years ago, assuming this was their permanent home. It was the wealthiest neighborhood in the city, resplendent with new single-family homes, square-cornered lawns and two-car garages. Most of the people in West Roxbury would describe themselves as middle class or even upper middle class. It was expensive to live here, but people thought it was worth it.

The neighborhood had a gracious air — far enough from the center of Boston so that often it seemed more a part of the suburbs than a part of the city. Perhaps because of the high cost of living in West Roxbury, less than 0.5 percent of the community was black.

Monday, September 12

Dear Journal. Well, the first day of school and already seven assignments. You're one of them. For creative writing class I have to record my impressions of the first six weeks of school. This should be interesting. I've been at this school now for what seems like forever. The first days are always the same. A lot of helter skelter as everyone gets their schedules squared away. A lot of getting reacquainted. A lot of rah, rah. To be perfectly honest, I'm a little tired of Latin, and am anxious to graduate. I don't really foresee anything new and exciting for this school year, but I'll keep you posted.

Thursday, September 15

So much for whoever said there's nothing new under the sun. In recent days, I've noticed something very new about Latin. Black students. Many black students. Of course I knew the court ordered more black kids into Latin, but I guess I never figured I'd notice that much. My mother warns of falling standards and all. Her argument seems to make sense, if in fact the kids are not high achievers. But it does seem only fair they should have a chance at a good education. Anyway, there are no problems yet. The black students just seem very bewildered. Of course there would never be any problems at Latin. That's not the Latin way.

Wednesday, September 20

More changes. I was assigned to tutor one of the black kids during my study period. It's OK with me, but my mother hit the roof. More fuel for her theory the standards are falling, or slipping, or whatever. His name is Jesse Stuart. He's a junior. He's far behind in math already, and his English is pretty bad. I don't know how much I can help him, but I've been told I have to. I'll give it a try. I hope I don't set him back. He seems like a nice enough kid.

Thursday, September 21

Well, Jesse has some real problems. He doesn't have any idea what he's doing in math. I got out a tenth grade book and he had trouble with basic algebra. I was going to try a ninth grade book, but couldn't find one. My mother says I should have tried a sixth grade book. I tried to explain some basic stuff to him, but I think he just got more confused. I wonder if we're really doing kids like Jesse a favor by putting all this pressure on him. He's really trying, but somewhere along the line, he wasn't taught much.

Friday, September 22

I feel like a bit of a crumb. I tried to get out of working with Jesse. He's just a hopeless case. But I've been told no one's hopeless and I have to keep trying. My mother wants to call the school and complain, but I won't let her. Jesse is an OK kid. He doesn't talk much. Last year he went to Dorchester High. He says he did good there, but is lost here. That's the truth. And he sure does feel out of place, but who can blame him?

Friday, September 29

Jesse is really hopeless. He failed one math pop quiz and got a D on an English paper this week. I looked at his English paper and I can see why. It was supposed to be about Mark Twain, but all he did was rewrite part of the chapter. He says he read the book, and I believe him. He's really trying hard, but he just doesn't seem to understand what he's reading. And his writing needs help. And this is just one black kid. I hate to think of how the others are doing. As much as I want Jesse to understand everything and do well, I'm beginning to wonder if my mother may be right. Kids like Jesse could drag down the reputation of Latin. But then the other side of all this is, what if Jesse just continued where he was? What type of education would he get? How would he ever know enough to survive in college? It's a real shame, because he tries so hard, and I really think he can do it. He's just never understood enough, or been taught enough.

Tuesday, October 3

A little bit of success with Jesse. I found out he doesn't read that hot. So I've started working with him on some basic reading skills. We just do a lot of reading now. I meet him before and after school, as well as my free period. He's really starting to understand, and boy is that good. I had forgotten what a joy it is just to read well. I guess I take a lot of my education for granted. I had a lot of chances Jesse just didn't have. But now Latin is really giving him a chance, and I don't think it's hopeless anymore. With some help, Jesse just may make it . . . even by Latin's standards.

Friday, October 5

Jesse is in real trouble. Someone gave him an old English paper to turn in for an essay assignment. Stupid move. The teacher immediately caught on, realizing it wasn't Jesse's work. The teacher is putting a lot of pressure on Jesse to find out who gave him the paper, but Jesse isn't telling, which is good for Jesse, as well as the other person. They suspend for stuff like that.

Wednesday, October 10

The flak over the essay has died down, and Jesse and I are now back full speed on the reading and math. He's learning about symbolism now. I explained to him how Huckleberry Finn isn't really a story about a kid floating down the river on a raft. That it all stood for something else. He not only caught on real fast, but found things in the story that had never occurred to me. He's really pretty smart. But tomorrow's the day. He's got an English test. Which reminds me, so do I.

Friday, October 12

Jesse got a C! I never saw anyone so happy. He said he's got a thick head, but it's all starting to soak in. I'm real happy for him, and the teachers have been supportive, thanking me for my help. And even Jesse has thanked me. I felt a little embarrassed, but it makes it all worthwhile. There have been a lot of black kids who have already dropped out. But I don't know if it's any more than the white kids who have left. Latin isn't easy for anyone. I'm not convinced school has to have so much pressure. But this is the best school in the city, and we've got to keep sending those graduates to the Ivy Leagues. I've already started filling out applications. What a drag. I can't help but wonder what Jesse will be doing the fall of his senior year.

Monday, October 15

My mother says where I talk about Jesse all the time, why don't I bring him home. No way. I don't think she's ready for that, and I don't think Jesse is either. I work well with him in school, but he has his friends, and I have mine. I hear he's got a real good sense of humor, but he's still pretty quiet around me. I'm afraid I intimidate him, being a senior and all. That's a shame. He shouldn't feel any less of a person than me. He just didn't get the right breaks. I really find it hard to believe it's his fault he didn't learn anything until he got here. Because he wants to learn. I hear from other kids that a lot of the black kids just don't care, and that's probably true. But it's also true for some white kids. Anyway, Jesse's coming along . . . rah rah Latin.

Tuesday, October 16

A funny thing happened today. A bunch of us were leaving school and this reporter and cameraman were standing out on the sidewalk doing a story. She asked us if she could interview us and we said sure. She asked if anything was different this year, and we all kind of stood there because, aside from more black kids, we couldn't think of anything that different. Then Benny pipes up and says, "Oh, yeah, there is something different. Mike Wright lost an election." Terrific.

The Lee School

"ANY CUSTOMERS?" Kathryn Ballou turned at the sound of Suzanne McNally's voice. McNally was the principal of the Lee Elementary School.

"Only a few," Ballou sighed. "Wonder what we did wrong."

"Not a thing. It wasn't you that scared the white parents off, it was this." McNally waved at the school behind them and the streets around it. The Lee School itself was one of the newest buildings in the whole city: clean red brick on the outside, brightly colored corridors on the inside leading to carpeted rooms arranged in "pods" — a modern design with a large central room connected to several smaller rooms around it. Kathryn Ballou, who taught art and music, liked to think of the arrangement as a flower spreading out.

The school had an up-to-date library, a well-equipped gym, music and drama rooms, a course schedule including art history and French, and even a swimming pool.

"No matter what you've got on the inside, what people look at is what you've got on the outside," McNally offered.

"Guess you're right." Ballou turned to look at the streets behind the Lee School. The school sat in the backyard of the Franklin Field housing project, in the heart of Boston's black community. Franklin Field had the reputation of being one of the most violent, debilitated projects in the city. The crime rate was high, the streets filthy.

In the late sixties it had been the scene of firebombings and riots. When fire engines tried to enter the project, fire fighters (the department was overwhelmingly white) would have to travel under police escort or face attack by brick-wielding blacks, angry at whites in general.

Even though the riots of the sixties had calmed, Franklin Field still looked a tragic mess. Much of it was burned out and abandoned. It was a place where no one would choose to live.

"You know," Kathryn Ballou said, "this school has got to be the nicest public building most of the people from that project have ever seen."

"Must be. It's one of the nicest ones I've seen. Too bad so many of their kids can't go here."

In this second year of desegregation, 1975, hundreds of black children from the project who had expected to attend the Lee, and were eager to, had instead been assigned to other schools as part of the desegregation plan. Their parents were angry and disappointed, and so were the children. The Lee was the most modern school in the black community. Now many black kids would again be refused admission here to make room for white kids — white kids, Ballou thought, who wouldn't come.

"Look at this," she pointed at the empty street in front of the school. "School's going to open in two weeks. This is our first open house and what happens? You get to greet the black parents, and you're swamped. I get to greet the white parents and I've had a grand total of seven!"

"Are they sending their kids?"

"Yeah, I think so. But still no first graders. Just the older kids. And of course three of the parents had their kids enrolled last year, so they can't wait to get their kids back in." Ballou sighed. "Isn't it a kick? Once we get them here, they're so impressed with the school they can't get enough of it. The problem is getting them here to even take a look."

"Back on the hustings tonight?"

"You got it," Ballou moaned. Like many other teachers at the Lee, Kathryn Ballou was determined to persuade as many white parents as possible to give the Lee a chance. The last three nights she had attended parents' meetings in West Roxbury. Another one was on tap for tonight.

"I've just got to convince them you can't tell a book by its cover," she said.

"That's not very original."

"I'm not feeling very original right now. I'm feeling damn discouraged that people can't recognize a good thing when they see it."

"Well, do your best."

* * *

The ride to West Roxbury always filled Ballou with a sense of serenity. Crickets chirped in the warm summer evening.

"You never hear crickets chirping in Roxbury," Ballou thought suddenly to herself. "Wonder why that is?" She shook her head at the vagaries of nature.

The boulevard swept through tree-lined streets of gracious single-family homes. Magnificent firs graced the stately well-groomed lawns.

"Must look like a picture postcard at Christmastime," she thought. Ballou had once dreamed of living in a community like this herself. She would fit in well with the affluent surroundings. She was a slender woman in her late twenties who enjoyed dressing stylishly. But, as her teaching career continued, she forgot about upper-class neighborhoods. She was now totally engrossed in the Lee Elementary School and making it work for white parents and children as well as black.

The meeting tonight was in an elegant brick-and-stone house in West Roxbury, an overwhelmingly white, middle- and upper-class section of Boston. It was the closest thing Boston had to a suburban neighborhood.

That's one of the problems, Ballou thought as she parked in the broad sweeping driveway. Like people in the suburbs, they don't have to send their kids to public schools. They can afford whatever they want. Private school, parochial school. She noticed several well-dressed women walking toward the front door. "Should be quite a job convincing them that a black-majority school in the heart of the black community is exactly what they've been looking for." She smiled to herself.

Nearly a dozen people sat in the large living room, a good turnout for meetings like this. Ballou and other teachers had organized as many parents' meetings as they could in West Roxbury in a desperate effort to persuade the parents to send their children to the Lee.

After greeting the hostess and shaking hands all around, Ballou took the center of the floor.

"Thank you all so much for coming. I know you're anxious about where your children have been assigned to school, and I'm here to tell you about the Lee and try to convince you to give it — and us — a chance."

She looked around the room at the polite faces. "You probably don't know that the Lee school is one big reason why the city is where it is today . . . one big reason a federal judge had to order busing to desegregate Boston's schools." The faces turned to her with new interest.

"Several years ago, the state department of education was leaning on the Boston School Committee to stop segregating its schools. Everyone knew the school committee was deliberately keeping black and white students apart, but this was the first time anyone had tried to force them to change."

"What was the department of education going to do?"

Ballou smiled. "They hit the school committee where it hurt, in the pocketbook. If Boston didn't start desegregating its schools, the state would withhold money."

"How much?"

Ballou paused dramatically. "Fifty-two million dollars." Someone in the back whistled.

"To keep the money flowing in, the school committee agreed to build a new multi-million-dollar school right between the white and black communities in Dorchester. Franklin Field Housing Project on one side would send black students; white Dorchester, which started at the opposite side of the Lee, would send white students. It was a beautiful plan. The Lee would be integrated naturally and all the kids could walk to school."

"What happened?"

"The white parents in Dorchester refused to send their kids."

"Did they have to walk through black neighborhoods?"

"Not at all. The Lee school sits smack in the middle of the white and black neighborhoods. The black kids walk through the black neighborhood on their side, and the white kids walk through the white neighborhood on their side.

"What was funny," Ballou started to chuckle, "is that some white parents convinced the school committee it was still too dangerous for their kids to walk, you know, crossing streets and all. So extra crossing guards were put out — and the most elaborate buses to move the kids a couple blocks. Big Mercedes buses, with plush seats, stereo music. The whole bit. But the buses arrived empty."

"So what was the problem?"

"The white parents were just afraid of the school's being

close to Franklin Field. They obviously didn't want their kids going to school with the black kids. And they wanted their children to attend the Fifield School right in their own neighborhood."

"That's gotta be one of the oldest schools in Boston!"

"It is. Dark classrooms. Old-fashioned desks bolted to the floor. Traditional teaching system. There's nothing wrong with that," Ballou hastened to explain. "It's just that most parents would welcome a chance to send their kids to a spanking-new school.

Her audience seemed captivated as the story unfolded. "So you had blacks in Franklin Field demanding that their kids get the seats in the Lee that the white kids didn't want. And the whites were demanding that they be allowed to send their kids to the Fifield. And the next night, despite its promise to the state to desegregate the schools, despite the likely consequences, the Boston School Committee went back on its word. The Lee became all black. The Fifield remained all white."

She paused. "And that was it for the school committee. That was the straw that broke the camel's back. From that day on, many people never again believed the Boston School Committee when it said it was acting in good faith."

She looked around the room, hoping she hadn't dwelled too long on the past. "To bring you quickly up to date: when Judge Garrity ordered Boston to desegregate its schools, that meant the Lee *had* to have fifty percent white, fifty percent black — whether the school committee liked it or not. And the fifty percent white are your children, from West Roxbury."

Ballou pretended not to notice that many people had stopped looking at her and instead were concentrating on the floor. They were reluctant to hear what she was going to say.

"The Lee school remains one of the finest elementary schools in Boston. There is no dispute about that. What I'm asking you today is to consider giving your child one of the finest educations the city — or the suburbs — can provide. Come to visit us! We'll show you around! The school and the staff sell the Lee themselves!"

The room was quiet. People still did not meet her stare. Ballou knew what they were thinking. She was proved right with the next question.

"You know," a woman in an easy chair near the front said, "I don't object at all to sending my children to school with black children. It's one of the reasons we stayed in the city instead of moving to the suburbs. We wanted our children to have urban experiences. The city can be a wonderful place for a child to live!" Several heads nodded in agreement.

"But it must be a positive experience," the woman continued. "No matter what you say, the Lee school is in one of the most dangerous parts of the city."

A man broke in. "It would be one thing to send your older kids on a bus through a bad section. High school kids, maybe. I could see that. But first graders? Second graders? I look at my boy, a six-year-old, and I think, My God, I can't send this little guy on a bus halfway across town! Where it may be dangerous! I'd never forgive myself if anything happened to him because I was trying to do what's right socially."

"We've never had any sort of racial incident at the Lee," Ballou said quietly. "Not in the school, not around the school."

The faces looked unconvinced. "I'm not saying it's a nice part of town," she said, "but I am saying that doesn't make any difference once you get inside that school. One thing I've learned in my several years of teaching is this: children are children when they're this young. Some are tougher to deal with than others, but that can be true whether they're black or white.

"Many, many of our black students come from strong families who are proud to send their children to school. They come each day all pressed and scrubbed. And of course" — she knew what they were thinking — "some of them don't. Some of them are raised by their mothers alone. Most of these kids are on welfare. And for many of our black kids, the family unit is no longer together."

She paused, waiting to drive her point home. "But in all honesty, you must admit that that's true even here in West Roxbury with its lovely homes and good incomes. You must admit there are plenty of perfectly fine children from broken families here. If you don't hold it against the kids you know from next door, don't hold it against the kids you don't know from Franklin Field."

Ballou was afraid she'd overstepped her mark, but she couldn't stop now. She turned to the man. "The young children, the first and second graders, are just the children we need! We have a hundred or so older children from West Roxbury who attended the Lee last year, but almost no younger ones. Until we see a first grader step off that bus from West Roxbury, we'll know we can never persuade white parents to put everything else aside and just consider the school."

She ended with her usual plea. "Please, come visit us. See what the school is like, and then decide. Please give us a chance. It's for your kids."

Kathryn Ballou shook her head as she listened to the children playing out back. Two girls, a white girl and a black girl, came running around the corner, holding hands and squealing. Ballou sent them back to the playground. Turning back to look for the bus, she thought of how alike these children actually were.

These kids come with the same tools, she thought to herself. They play the same games, watch the same television programs, laugh the same laughs, cry over the same things.

She watched the last of the walkers — the children who walked from the housing project — come across the playground. He was swinging a plastic bat. He had for the most part outgrown his overalls, or they had shrunk from too many washings. Ballou knew him: Andrew, a quiet kid in second grade, who was already reading at the fourth-grade level.

Ballou smiled, as she watched a group of white and black kids run toward Andrew. "These kids just weren't born different from each other," she mumbled to herself. "Here they have the same desks, the same pencils and crayons, the same books. They sing the same songs. It just doesn't matter what their bedrooms look like at home."

"Talking to yourself again, Kathryn?" Ballou was startled to hear McNally's voice in back of her. She swung around. "Well, it does get pretty lonely out here. Year after year, waiting for the white kids."

"I guess you're right," McNally laughed. "How we doing this year?"

"Not bad for the first day. The buses have a good number of kids."

"Better than previous years, that's for sure," said McNally. "I think if this last bus is full, we'll have about a hundred and fifty kids from West Roxbury . . . and we should pick up more in the next few weeks."

"That is good — a new record," said Ballou excitedly. But she could tell McNally was disappointed. Almost five hundred white kids had been assigned. If the seats weren't filled by whites, they would stand empty.

McNally smiled, then sighed and turned back toward the school. "It's not bad, considering where we began, what we had to deal with. But that still only gives us about six hundred kids. Over four hundred seats go empty at this school. What a waste, a loss for so many kids."

"But remember one thing," shouted Ballou as the principal reached for the door. "We've never lost a child once we got him."

Ms. McNally smiled and gave the victory sign.

Ballou turned just in time to see the last yellow bus coming down Talbot Avenue, headed for the Lee. She felt her excitement returning as she noticed how full it seemed.

As the bus pulled in front, she returned the waves and shouts of fourth and fifth graders who were returning from last year. No, they never had lost a kid. It was the magic of the Lee.

The kids bounded down the steps, swinging lunch pails, shouting at Ballou . . . had she seen Sam or Cliff or Bonnie: all children Ballou knew had walked from the project this morning and were waiting in the playground.

Suddenly her attention was drawn to the school bus door. Perched at the top step, looking absolutely petrified, was a young boy, a very young boy. He was a first grader. Ballou reached for him to help him down. But he was holding the hand of a friend, another first grader. And in back of them, two more, with an older sister whom Ballou recognized from last year's third grade.

Ballou felt a smile come across her face. She wanted to jump up and down in joy. If only these innocent children knew how happy they had made her, and the whole school. It was all worthwhile, now.

She helped the children down the steps, took their hands, touched their cheeks, smiling and chatting the whole time, telling them not to be frightened, it's just the first day of school.

Tony

THE FIRE ALARM rang out just as classes were changing for the last period. It couldn't have been worse timing. If students had still been in their classrooms, instead of in the halls, the teachers could have prevented the students from going outside.

Tony and several other black students were in the gym when they heard it. They grabbed their books and jackets and headed out the door as the public-address system crackled to life.

"This is a false alarm. Please return to your classrooms. Repeat. There is no fire. This is a false alarm."

By this time, Tony was practically out the front door.

"What the hell," he said to his friend Chandler. "Let's just wait outside and make sure. Something might happen."

The broad, gray-brick pavilion of English High School was filled with milling students. Some leaned against the large cement planters that dotted the different levels of the stone plaza. Tony turned to see more students, laughing now, pour out of the tall, modern building. English High was Boston's newest school, with sleek, spacious classrooms, art and drama centers, well-equipped labs, even a swimming pool. It was the only public school with escalators, which carried almost two thousand students up and down the ten floors of classrooms each day.

"Hey, man, let's go back in. Ain't nothin' doin' out here." Chandler turned toward the entrance.

"Oh, yeah? Look over there."

The headmaster was in the street in front of the school, trying to shoo students back toward the building. Photographers from local television stations and newspapers recorded his efforts. The headmaster appeared on the brink of success when a knot of several dozen black students broke away and set off down the street at a run.

"They're headin' for the projects," Tony realized, looking toward Mission Hill a few blocks away and the housing project that was his home. "Gonna tear 'em up for the Six O'Clock News."

Trouble rarely flared at English High School itself, partly because it was located in an area of hospitals and colleges and not in an established neighborhood. No one felt the school was on their turf so that they had to protect it from outsiders.

Also, students had signed up voluntarily to attend English, even if it meant a bus ride across the city, so there was much less resentment about forced busing than there was at many other schools. The students wanted to go to English because it had the city's best art and music programs. The same judge who ordered desegregation ordered several high schools, like English, to offer special classes in one field or another. These schools were called magnet schools. The idea was that the programs would be so good they would attract black and white students voluntarily from all over the city, and the schools could be integrated without forcing anyone to attend them. So far, in this second year of desegregation, the idea had worked.

"You wanna go?" Chandler gestured toward the students, now almost out of sight.

"Are you kiddin'? Come on. Who needs it."

"School's almost out anyway. Let's just head for practice."

"Yeah," said Tony eagerly. It was the high point of his day. During his first three years at Dorchester High, he had lettered every year as a fullback and also played varsity basketball and track. Probably not big enough, or fast enough, to play pro ball, Tony thought he'd have a good shot at college ball. That's why he transferred to English for his senior year. His coach at Dot High had persuaded him he'd have a better chance at a scholarship if he graduated from English than from Dorchester. A football scholarship was his ticket to a college education.

"First week of practice is always the toughest," Tony said as they walked toward the practice field.

"I hear ya."

"Especially here."

"Yeah, yeah."

"You guys on the team always so tight?"

"Hey. We all came in together last year, man. White and black, you know. Worked through all the shit last year. Now we're sailin'. Puts you in a bad spot, you dig?"

"Yeah. I'm the new kid on the block." Tony thought that he got all the dumb luck. His position, fullback, was the same one played by the team captain, Jack Kerr, a tall blond senior elected unanimously by the team the year before. The other guys were happy to see Tony, but they were upset that he was so determined to grab the starting slot and bench their captain.

"Kerr hate me because I'm after his job or 'cause I'm black?"

"Cause you're after his job. He doesn't operate the other way. Least he never has."

"Ain't nothin' personal," Tony muttered under his breath as he pulled on his helmet. "Good somebody here likes me." Coach Mahard had been delighted that a star fullback from another high school had transferred to English High. And the blacks on the team had been friendly, many of them advising him that he was in a lousy position: the better Tony was, the more likely that Kerr would ride the bench. The whole team would feel sorry for Kerr if he got pushed aside in his senior year.

Tony and Chandler took their places at the fifteen-yard line for tackling practice.

"You talked to the coach yet about startin'?" Chandler asked.

"Yeah. He says I've got it for the first game."

"Ooooooh. Jackie-boy's gonna be rippin'."

Tony shrugged. He had as much right to the job as Jack.

He stepped into line for his turn at the dummy. He watched the line of players in front of him crouch low to the ground. They looked like one big shoulder pad. The coach shouted. Tony watched them sprint several yards to a row of oblong dummies. They dug their shoulders in deep as the players supporting the tough canvas forms tried to hold their ground.

When his turn came, Tony ground his cleats into the turf and tensed his muscles, listening intently for the coach's shout: *"Go!"*

Tony raced for the dummy, feeling his senses quicken. Even in practice, he got excited as soon as he swung into action. It was one of the reasons, Coach Mahard told him, that he'd start on Saturday. Tony was just plain hungry.

"Ummpf!" Tony tucked his shoulder deep into the dummy and dug in hard with his feet. He could feel the player on the other side grunt under the weight of his attack.

"Cool it, rookie." Tony looked up to see Jack Kerr on the other side of the dummy, struggling to keep it in place. They were both tall, about six feet, but where Jack was just big, Tony was muscular. He worked at it.

"Who you callin' rookie?"

"You, rookie. Heard you're startin' Saturday."

"No hard feelings?"

"Are you kiddin'? That's *my* job. I paid my dues here." Jack took off his helmet and spat on the ground. "For your information, I don't like being bounced by the likes of you."

Tony thrust his face inches from Jack's. "Don't mess with me, man. I mean it."

"Hope you fall on your ass." Jack spat again.

Tony grabbed him by the front of his jersey, catching Jack off guard.

"You're about to fall on your white ass right here," he hissed, twisting the material tighter.

"All right, you two!"

Still holding Jack's jersey, Tony turned to see Coach Mahard coming toward them on the run. The rest of the players suddenly realized what was happening and stopped in their tracks.

"You think we got time for this?" Coach Mahard demanded. "The first game is this Saturday, and you two guys got to play nursery school?"

He looked from one to the other. "OK, who started this?"

Tony and Jack stood silently.

"All right!" the coach barked. "You're both benched for this game. You know the rules here. Discipline and sportsmanship. Everyone works together."

Tony's heart sank. Benched! He turned to walk back to the school.

"You fool!" Tony spun around to see Chuck Wilson,

the black assistant coach. "You think you're accomplishing anything by this?" He grabbed Tony's arm and dragged him aside.

"He was messin' with me," Tony complained.

"I don't give a good goddamn. You just keep your cool."

Tony started to answer when Wilson cut him off.

"You think it was easy for Jack to get bumped? It's his senior year too, you know."

"He doesn't like blacks."

"Get outa here! Look at that field," Wilson gestured to the playing field behind them. "Black guys and white guys, right? What do you expect. You should waltz in here your first week and bump the team captain and win a popularity contest? Just be cool, man, understand where he's comin' from."

Tony jerked his arm away. "This is important to me, man," he said angrily. "I'm countin' on this year to pay my way for the next four. Can you dig *that*?"

"Hey, it's important to everybody. Meanwhile, sucker" — Coach Wilson turned to leave — "you and Jack are both benched for the next game. What's *that* gonna do for your college education?"

Tony clenched his teeth as he watched Wilson walk back to the field. Coach Wilson was right. He'd gotten off to a bad start with the coaches and many of the players. It was the last thing he wanted to do. In fact, he'd been trying to butter the coaches up, not only because he was new, but because he'd wanted that starting slot so badly.

"Tony! Ain't you up yet?" His mother's voice rang out shrilly from the kitchen. Already he could hear cartoons blaring in the living room where Roland and Bobby were sitting, eating their cereal, their eyes fixed on the screen in front of them.

Tony reviewed what he had to do. Walk Roland to the bus stop to catch a ride to the suburb of Newton, where he attended first grade. Then back home to make sure Bobby had his lunch and a change of clothes before he went two doors away to the baby-sitter's. Remind Mom it was food-stamp day and tell her to sign up for WIC: "Women, Infants and Children." It was a program that gave low-income women money to buy nutritious food if they were pregnant or had little kids. Tony's mother was due in three months.

He sighed as he pulled on his pants. His own father was only a dim memory; he'd moved out when Tony was two and had never been heard from since. He wished his mother weren't having this new baby, but they'd never discussed it.

Tony paused at his bedroom door and looked around at his room. It was small and dark, his rumpled bed pushed up against one grimy wall, the shallow closet next to it filled with peeling paint and a family of cockroaches. The Mission Hill housing project was considered the worst in the city. A reputation, Tony thought, it well deserved. He couldn't wait to get out. He saw college as his ticket to a better life. Life "on the outside," as he put it. He was counting on an athletic scholarship to get him there. Doing well this year at English High was crucial.

At first, Tony's mother resisted the idea of college. She was counting on a weekly paycheck from him when he finished high school. But once she was persuaded that college was a good idea for Tony, she became his biggest supporter. She even signed up her younger boys for Metco, the program that bused city kids to suburban schools.

"No, my boys ain't spending the rest of their lives in these projects," Tony's mother would lecture her neighbors. "Lord knows I'll never get out, but they sure as hell will."

For some reason, Tony believed his mother's prophecy. He and his brothers would get out. But his mother, no. She seemed to belong in the projects. She had learned to survive, to accept it. In much the same way, she had raised them not to accept it, not to belong.

He shook his head as he walked into the kitchen. His mother was grabbing cornbread squares out of the too-hot oven.

"Christ, Ma! Haven't you ever heard of a potholder?"

"You handle the football. I'll handle the damn cornbread." She slammed the oven door, then her voice softened.

"Can't come to the game Saturday, honey. Girls and me goin' downtown."

"That's OK," Tony said, secretly relieved. He helped himself to a bowl of cereal. "Shouldn't smoke, you know, Ma."

"Get off my back, boy."

"OK."

"I been smokin' since before you was born."

"You musta started pretty early then," he laughed. He knew his mother was only sixteen when he was born. "Musta been smokin' in the cradle."

She laughed, in a good mood now. "Smokin' and more, professor, smokin' and more!"

The school day seemed to drag. Tony's mind wandered. He couldn't tell English from art history today. His mind was busy imagining the first game on Saturday, the quarterback slapping the ball into his hands. He could almost feel it.

He snapped back to reality. He wasn't playing Saturday. Unless Coach Mahard had a change of heart, of course, and that wasn't likely. Tony doodled moodily in his notebook.

After school he wandered aimlessly through the nearly deserted hallways. Usually he liked to get to practice early and run a couple of laps to loosen up. He was so keyed up the day before a game that he had to keep himself busy every second or he'd fly right out of his head. Today, though, he didn't seem to know what to do with himself.

Tony glanced into the classrooms as he sauntered by.

Here and there a teacher and a student sat huddled over a book. Most teachers at English were pretty good about helping you after school if you asked. He could see one classroom with three kids sitting in it, their hands folded in front of them. They were probably in trouble for acting up in class, Tony thought as he strolled by.

He nearly passed the last classroom on the corridor without glancing in, then stopped in his tracks. Inside the empty room, he could see a girl smacking handfuls of clay over a bunch of sticks. Tony took a step closer as he tried to figure out what she was doing. Smack! Smack! The clay clung to the sticks, which were glued into some sort of structure Tony couldn't figure out. It looked for all the world as if she were piling clay onto an odd-looking box made out of sticks.

"All right!" Tony declared, striding into the room. "I give up. What are you doing in here?" He was startled when he realized the girl was one of the cheerleaders. Today, though, she wore a printed smock over her clothes instead of a uniform, and a bandana held back her long brown hair.

"I'm creating," she said, squinting critically at the mess of sticks and clay in front of her. Suddenly she turned to Tony. "Put her there!" She stuck out her hand, coated with clay.

"OK," he said agreeably, clenching her gooey hand in his own. He squeezed it hard, chuckling as the clay oozed between her fingers.

"Yuk." She drew her hand out of his.

"You asked for it."

She turned back to her project. Tony shuffled his feet.

"So. I'm Tony Dawson."

"Annie Sullivan."

"Cheerleader, right?"

"You got it."

"Saw you on the field the other day."

"I was waiting for my boyfriend."

"Yeah?"

"Jack Kerr. You guys were pushin' each other around."

"Nothin' personal," Tony said defensively.

"Give him a break, will you?"

"Give *him* a break! I won that job fair and square and he's cryin' like a baby about it! How come everybody's blamin' me? He's the one started giving me shit about it!"

Annie just shrugged. "He's a popular guy. People hate to see him get bounced."

Tony was about to respond when the door opened.

"Ready?" Jack Kerr walked in.

He stopped short when he saw Tony.

"What the hell are you doin' here?"

"I go to school here, man. Any objections?"

"Yeah. Get outa my life."

"Just back off, will ya?" Tony tried to force himself to be calm. "Look. I won that starting job. I'm sorry it was you who got bounced, but that's the way it goes. Nothin' you can do about it but beat me on the playing field. If you can." He stared evenly at Kerr, who was glaring at him, the veins standing out on his neck. It crossed his mind that Kerr might try to hit him. Tony sort of hoped he would. It would be a good excuse to slam the guy.

The door of the art room banged shut. Tony, Annie, and Jack spun around to see three blacks walking slowly toward them. The biggest one nodded at Tony. "Hey, brother." Then he nodded toward Jack.

"Hear this mother's givin' you some grief. Need some help?"

Tony thought he recognized one of them, but not the other two. They seemed too old to be in school.

"The situation's under control," Tony said quickly. He didn't like Jack very much, but these guys were bad trouble. This type of brother ruled in every project in the city. He wondered how they had gotten into the school.

"Think we oughta teach John-boy a lesson? Let him know who's the head man at this school?" The big one was doing the talking again. The other two just nodded.

Tony realized there was only one way to get rid of them. "I'll handle it, man. If I need any help, I'll let you know."

"That's smooth. I can read that. See you around, man." They slapped hands. The three left. Jack turned to Annie.

"Do you believe that? Wait 'til I tell Mike and the other guys!"

"Are you crazy? You wanta start a war in this school? Let 'em go." Annie gestured at the door. "They're nothin' but trouble."

"She's right," Tony picked up his books as Jack stared at him in surprise. "I'm goin' to practice."

*   *   *

The locker room smelled sweaty and close. It was full of boys suiting up for practice. Tony spotted the center, a guy he'd gotten to know a little, straightening his shoulder pads near his open locker.

"Hey, Jimmy."

The boy looked at Tony but didn't say anything.

"Hey, what's the matter?"

Jimmy shook his head, his blond hair falling across his eyes.

"No I mean it, man, what's goin' on?"

"You just cost us the game tomorrow night. That's all."

"What do you mean?"

"You and Jack both benched, right? We gotta put in Andy. He barely made the team this year." He turned back to his locker.

"Hey! He was the one who started it!"

"He was just givin' you a rough time. You're the one who started fightin'. You should have let him go."

"Let's let you go," a voice shouted from several lockers away. Tony heard a few others chuckle. He lunged toward the speaker. Out of the corner of his eye he saw two other blacks move in that direction, too.

One of them arrived first and crashed the white player against a locker. Everyone started to shove and shout. At that moment someone shouting louder than everyone else began pushing his way through the crowd of players. It was Coach Mahard. His face was beet red. He was so mad he was shaking.

"That's it. That's it. I'm not going to have this on my

team. This is English High, not Charlestown or Southie." He was surrounded by players and kept spinning around, glaring at all the faces.

"Don't bother suiting up today. There's no practice. And tomorrow, there will be no game unless you guys get your heads on straight. You understand? Don't come to the stadium unless you're going to be gentlemen and forget this fighting."

The locker room was dead silent. Coach Mahard stared at his players. "Those of you who have been playing with me for four years know I never go back on my word. And this is the word: Any player seen fighting or arguing with another player . . . or trying to start something . . . is off the team. Off. Permanently."

The coach pushed his way silently through the players. Tony couldn't remember ever seeing anyone so mad. When the coach was out of the room, the players just stood there for a moment, not looking at each other. A few muttered to themselves as they put their equipment away and walked toward the door. No one looked at Tony.

Outside Tony searched the sky for clouds. "Should be a nice day for the game tomorrow." Damn it, he wanted to play so badly.

"I wanna talk to you, Tony." It was Chuck Wilson, the black assistant coach.

"Yeah?"

"You gotta stop takin' everything personally, man."

"I don't do that."

"Yes, you do. Anytime anybody looks at you cross-eyed you jump on 'em."

"I don't let anybody call me nigger."

"Nobody's callin' you nigger," Coach Wilson said in exasperation. "And if they did, I'd be the first one to boot them outa here. We don't stand for that crap. Every time one of the guys gives you a rough time you fly off the handle. It's nothin' to do with race, man. They're just upset that you're causin' so much trouble."

"I didn't mean to," Tony said defensively.

"I know that, man. But you've got to learn to let things ride, you know? Somebody says something you don't like, just be cool. Don't start throwing them all over the locker room."

"Yeah. I hear ya."

"Look, you came here as a senior and that's rough. And you're taking away the starting position from the captain of the team. And that's rough. Then guys start ridin' you a little and you blow up. Just let it pass. You understand?"

Tony nodded. He already felt terrible about the way things had worked out. He didn't want them to get any worse.

"So you just lay back a little, OK?" Wilson patted his arm. "You're your own worst enemy, man."

"Yeah." He didn't want to talk about it anymore.

It was one of the worst games Tony had ever seen. The stadium was filled with disappointed English High fans. They were losing. Badly. Coach Mahard had stuck by his promise. Tony and Jack just warmed their rear ends on the bench. The coach didn't even look at them. Almost no one talked to Tony. Andy, the third stringer, was as bad as everyone had expected. He fumbled twice and barely gained eleven yards the entire game. English lost by twenty-four points.

In the locker room later, Coach Mahard called the team together. "There's not much I can say. You played terribly. I probably coached terribly. This is what happens when you don't play as a team."

His voice dropped. "We could be having our best season ever. But we've got to do it together. I'll see you at practice Monday . . . as a team."

Tony hopped from one foot to the other. He was so excited he could hardly hold still. All week he had been building up to today's game. The guys had all been a little cool to him, but he had just kept to himself. Now that the big game with East Boston High was about to start, he was nervous with anticipation. He really loved to play football.

English won the toss. They would receive.

Coach Mahard shouted over his shoulder. "OK, Kerr, get in there." Tony's heart sank as he watched Jack lope toward the huddle on the field. He was so disappointed he felt as if he could cry. A whole week of hard practice and he wasn't even in the game.

"That's what you get," the player next to him muttered. Tony whirled and was about to grab him when he caught himself. No matter what, he wasn't going to fly off the handle again. He turned back to watch the play.

It was a handoff to Jack. Tony watched in grudging admiration as Jack twisted and plunged through a small hole in the line. A gain of six yards. The guy wasn't bad.

"Dawson, come here." It was the coach. "Next play you go in. I'll tell you what play to take in." Tony snapped his chin strap nervously. He couldn't wait to get into the game. His heart was pounding.

"OK, it's a handoff to you." Coach Mahard pushed Tony toward the field. He raced toward the huddle. Without thinking about it, he held out his hand to the player running toward the sidelines. It was an old habit. The player coming toward him gave it a good slap and said, "Go!"

Not until Tony was crouched in the huddle did he remember the player he had replaced was Jack.

He lined up behind the quarterback and listened intently as he barked out the signals. "Red forty-one! Red forty-one! Hut!" The quarterback swirled and jammed the football into Tony's waiting hands.

Tony took two quick steps to the right. He was going to try to follow the big right guard. He heard the smack of helmet on helmet as the guard tried to hold back tacklers and let Tony squeeze through. Tony raced past him and saw a sparkle of daylight ahead. He jumped over a player on the ground and ran hard, straight ahead. He could see East Boston's safety man running down the field toward him, trying to make the tackle. Tony spun to the left. He felt a hand grab him from the back. He hadn't realized the guy was there. He tried to give him a straight arm, but the guy slowed him down enough for the safety to land on him hard.

"Ummmpf!" Tony lay on the ground, the ball still clutched in his hands. Four hundred pounds of East Boston football players on top of him. He peeked toward the sideline markers. An eighteen-yard gain! He was elated.

"Hey, man, get off him." Tony heard one of his teammates shouting at the East Boston guys to untangle. "That was great!" He held out his hand to pull Tony to his feet. Tony tossed the ball to one of the officials and dashed back to the huddle. Guys were slapping each other on the back.

"We're cookin', man, we're cookin'." Tony slapped hands excitedly with the right guard.

They crouched together quickly and heard the next play. It would go to the halfback. Tony would block for him. He wasn't disappointed not to get the ball again right away. He just wanted to play.

"Red sixteen! Red sixteen! Hut! Hut!"

Tony raced into the line, the halfback with the football right behind him. He jammed his arms together and plowed into the East Boston tackle in front of him. Tony was trying to push him to the left. The guy was big and strong, but Tony held. The halfback slipped by them. Ten yards! Another first down!

Tony practically danced back to the huddle. Everyone

was slapping everyone else on the back. They really had a head of steam up. "Kerr in, Dawson out," the center said, as he spotted Jack Kerr racing toward the huddle, bringing in the next play.

Tony dashed toward the sidelines, slapping hands with Kerr on the way. This time he didn't think twice about it.

"You'll go in next play," Coach Mahard said. "We'll keep trading you two off. Keeps you fresh. Nice play, Tony."

Tony was pleased and still all keyed up about the game. He turned back to the field. It was going to be a pass. His hands clenched and unclenched as the quarterback dropped back to pass. He almost felt as if he were in there himself, dropping back to protect the quarterback.

It was a beautiful pass. Long and spiraling. Tony held his breath. There was a big pileup in the end zone. The tight end caught it! Touchdown English!

Pandemonium! Tony jumped up and down, grabbing the excited players running off the field to the sidelines. Everyone was whooping and hugging.

"Great play, man, great play!" He smacked the hands of the receiver.

"You too, man. Good to have you on our team."

"Hey," Tony found himself happy to say, "glad to be here!"

Vinnie

OH, VINNIE, I forgot to tell you . . ." Mrs. Macioce touched her son's shoulder as she placed a bowl of steaming vegetables in front of him. "Scott stopped by this afternoon. Wanted to know why you weren't at practice the last two days. I thought you were."

"Not at practice?" His father looked up from his dinner in surprise.

Vinnie glanced from his father to his mother. He knew they weren't going to like what he had to say, but he had no choice.

"Things aren't going that well at the high school."

"I thought you couldn't wait to get back. Now you been there three days and you don't like it?"

Vinnie toyed with his mashed potatoes. His father was right. He had looked forward to returning to school with the "Townies," as people from Charlestown are called. But it just wasn't working out the way he had expected.

"I thought you were dyin' to go to Charlestown High."

"I was."

"I thought after last year at Roxbury High you'd be glad to be back."

"I thought so, too."

Last year when Vinnie was assigned to eleventh grade at Roxbury High, he was furious. It was an all-black school right in the middle of Boston's black community. Vinnie grew up in Charlestown and most people there were against busing whites out, or blacks in.

But if Vinnie was unhappy about having to take a bus over to school in Roxbury, that was about the extent of his displeasure. He didn't yet have anything against blacks, even though most of his neighbors had no use for blacks. But Vinnie had been brought up in a home that took no stock in racial animosity. His father simply didn't share much of the sentiment in Charlestown, even though he himself was a native Townie. He worked alongside black people at the navy shipyard south of Boston and often insisted, "They work just as hard as any white man."

Vinnie's father was different from many of his Charlestown neighbors in another way. He really wanted his kids to go to college. You'd never hear him talking in sarcastic tones about the "college boys." Going to college meant finishing high school.

Now Vinnie laughed. "Remember how you convinced me to go to Roxbury last year? You said, 'Give it a try! Probably lots of kids from Charlestown will be there!' That first day! I remember standing at the bus stop sayin' to myself, 'Dad says lots of white kids will be there, he must know what he's talkin' about.' First I wondered how everybody else was gettin' there since nobody was on the bus but me."

"A little slow, are you?" his mother asked.

"Whew!" Vinnie shook his head. "Then I got off at Roxbury High and saw only three other white kids outa three hundred! It was about a hundred black kids to each white kid! And the next day, one of the white kids dropped out!"

"Good thing you were afraid to walk home from Roxbury or you probably would have left right then and there," his father said.

"It turned out to be not so bad," Vinnie said, returning to his dinner.

"Not so bad for you, maybe," his mother said. "You shoulda been stuck at home. It got so I wouldn't even go near Luca's Market for fear of runnin' into that woman."

Neither Vinnie nor his father had to ask for further identification. Their next door neighbor, Mrs. Fitzsimmons, was a virulent busing opponent and seldom missed an opportunity to lecture Mrs. Macioce on the dangers of sending her child to Roxbury. That Mrs. Fitzsimmons lived next door was bad enough, in Mrs. Macioce's view. That she was a checkout clerk at the nearest neighborhood market was unbearable. A simple trip to the store for milk would grow into an extended debate over busing.

Many of their neighbors were more curious than angry about Vinnie's decision to attend Roxbury High. Their own children, who had also been assigned to Roxbury, either attended parochial schools or were sitting the school year out. Vinnie still hung out with some of them, but they weren't as close as before. And once when he'd gotten into a fight, the other guy had called him "nigger lover." A lot of them thought Vinnie was a nice guy but a little odd.

All summer, Vinnie had planned on returning to Roxbury High for his senior year. Then, just three weeks before school, he learned he could transfer back to Charlestown High. He grabbed the chance.

"So what's the problem at Charlestown High?" his father asked.

"I don't know how to put it."

"Well try, will you?" Vinnie could tell his father was running out of patience.

"Charlestown High stinks."

Vinnie's father looked silently at his wife and shook his head.

"I don't know about you, kid."

"What do you mean?"

"You been back three days and you can say it stinks? You went there ninth and tenth grade and you didn't say it stinks then."

"Well, I know more now."

"You're gettin' so wise in your old age." Vinnie's father concentrated on his dinner for a moment. "So what's too stinky for you?"

"I don't know," Vinnie was exasperated, finding it so

difficult to express himself. "It's just at Charlestown they don't expect you to do anything but graduate and get a job and live in Charlestown all your life."

"You could do worse."

"I could do better, too."

His father smiled. "You could go to Roxbury High and graduate and get a job and live in Roxbury all your life?"

"It's just that there's all this stuff goin' on at Roxbury and nothing special goin' on at Charlestown."

"Like what?"

"Like, you know, those classes I liked so much that the guy from Harvard set up?"

"Vinnie," his mother spoke up sharply, "I hope you don't think we can afford to send you to Harvard."

"Naw. Although," he glanced at his father, "Roxbury gets lots of scholarships."

"Hmrmph." Vinnie couldn't tell if he'd scored a point or not.

"Mother" (Vinnie's father always addressed his wife as "Mother"), "Harvard was involved because the court said it had to work with Roxbury High. The judge must have figured it'd look better to more white kids if Harvard was involved."

"Too bad he figured wrong," she said.

"But it's really better there!" Vinnie felt he had to speak out. "I mean it! The stuff we're doin' this year at Charlestown I did *last year* at Roxbury!"

"So why don't you go back to Roxbury?" his father suggested mildly, pushing away from the table.

"What?" Vinnie couldn't believe his ears. It was the point he'd been leading up to.

"Why don't you go back to Roxbury?" his father repeated, searching in his pocket for a toothpick and looking around the kitchen for the evening paper. He found it, yawned, and wandered into the living room.

"Oh, Vinnie," his mother sighed, "here we go again."

The hardest part was standing outside Charlestown High again. Vinnie hadn't realized when he made his decision that he'd have to return here to get the headmaster's signature on his transfer papers. He dreaded the explanations.

"Hey, Vinnie!"

"Hey, Scott!" They slapped hands.

"Where you been?"

"Round and about."

"No, really. You droppin' off the team?"

"Yeah. Guess so."

"How come?"

"You know, other stuff's come up." Vinnie hoped he could leave it all vague. He was nervous enough about telling the headmaster. He shuddered to think of what the guys would say if they knew he was returning to Roxbury High voluntarily. Call him names. Push him around, maybe. Better they should just find out later, or not at all. Vinnie knew they'd find out about him when he just stopped coming to school, but he wasn't going to think about that. Right now, he just wanted to get the paper signed and get out.

"You sure you want to do this?" the assistant headmaster squinted at the transfer paper, then at Vinnie.

"Yeah."

"Why?"

"I just do."

The assistant looked at him silently, perhaps hoping Vinnie would offer more. But Vinnie had already decided the less he said, the better.

The man sighed. "OK, kid. But don't try to get back in later. There's lots in line for your seat here."

"Right." Vinnie grabbed the paper and headed for the door.

The next morning Vinnie walked through the empty, clean streets of Charlestown, thankful he had an early bus pickup. What he didn't need was to bump into some of his friends heading for Charlestown High.

The bus was a few minutes late, as usual. At first he was afraid it wasn't even going to stop. Finally it did, about twenty-five yards past him.

"Roxbury High?" hollered the driver as he opened the doors.

"Yeah." Vinnie climbed on.

The driver looked at him incredulously. "I've been comin' by here for a week, and you're my first customer. You goin' to check it out for a day?"

"Already checked it out. I'll be goin' there 'til June."

Vinnie settled into his seat as the driver watched him through the rear-view mirror. Vinnie knew the driver thought he was nuts, but Vinnie didn't care.

Vinnie was the only passenger as they rode through the tidy streets of Charlestown, but in the Chinatown section of Boston, they picked up a dozen Asian students. Vinnie brightened when he recognized Jeanne Wu, who had been in most of his classes last year.

"Hey! Wu!" Everyone called her by her last name.

"Hey Vinnie! What are you doin' on this bus?" She sat down next to him, all smiles.

"I'm comin' back."

"What happened to Charlestown?"

"It's still there. Last I saw, anyway."

"I mean the high school, stupid." She whacked him on the arm.

"Oh, it's there too."

"I mean what happened to you going to Charlestown High School? And answer me or I'm gonna shake your teeth out!"

Vinnie laughed. "Decided this joint was better."

"Good for you."

"Yeah."

"Gonna be hell to pay in Charlestown?"

"I don't think so."

"How come?"

"Three years ago when busing first started, maybe. Hell, they used to smash windows of people who sent their kids to school at all! Even if it was right in Charlestown! But people just kinda gave up on doin' anything about it."

"Oh, yeah? Then how come this bus isn't full of kids from Charlestown?"

"Hey! Gettin' used to it doesn't mean they like it. Also doesn't mean people from Charlestown are gonna send their kids to Roxbury. Ever. Just means they're not gonna burn your house down if you decide to go."

"Still bet you're not too popular there."

"Probably not. It's one thing to get sent here by the judge. It's another thing to choose it. Any white kids this year?"

"Naw. About the same as last."

"Damn. I was hopin' that people would realize there wasn't any trouble here."

"Has nothin' to do with the school, Vinnie."

Wu had a point, Vinnie thought, as he looked out the window at the tattered Roxbury streets. Lots of white people were just plain scared of this neighborhood. He stared at broken windows, a car stripped of everything that could be sold, and the charred windowsills of a gutted apartment building.

The crime rate was high, and for a while during desegregation troubles, white people had been afraid even to ride through this section of town. Since black people weren't safe riding through South Boston or Charlestown, Vinnie thought, white people figured they wouldn't be safe in the black neighborhoods. But Vinnie had never had any trouble here, although he made a point of being out of the area when it grew dark.

As the bus approached the vanilla-colored high school, the neighborhood grew much classier — nicer than parts of his own — large multicolored houses with small lawns. A single policeman lounged against the entrance to the school, a coffee cup in his hand.

Wu nudged Vinnie.

"You'd never see that in Charlestown."

"What do you mean?"

"You've got to have a whole army there. This guy could retire. The most he did last year was give directions."

Vinnie suddenly felt defensive about Charlestown. "There's not that much trouble there anymore."

"Oh, yeah? Then how come I saw a picture on the front page of the paper yesterday of a bunch of Charlestown kids leaving school to march to City Hall? Said they wanted to protest busing."

"Protest busing, my ass. They wanted to get outa school."

"Nothin' happened to 'em," Wu pointed out as they stepped off the bus. "City councillor even came out to meet them. Served 'em donuts. If we did that," she swept her arms out to indicate the crowd of black and Asian students swarming into the high school, "they'd be scared shitless! They'd call out the national guard!"

"Vinnie! Vinnie!" shouted the middle-aged white man

at the school's entrance. It was Charlie Ray, the Roxbury High headmaster and one of the few administrators in the system who knew the names of all his students. He was all smiles.

"Isn't it wonderful! I heard you were coming back!" He pumped Vinnie's hand and guided him into the school.

"Yeah, guess Roxbury High's gonna be my alma mater."

"How about your mom and dad, Vinnie?" His voice dropped.

"My dad doesn't care. Says do what I want. My mom would like me to stay in Charlestown, but you know . . . ." He shrugged.

"Well, we're honored to have you back. Bet you want to get back in the Harvard program you were in last year." Mr. Ray knew that Vinnie was an easygoing boy, but more serious about his studies than many others.

As Vinnie and Mr. Ray walked down the corridor, they heard the sound of someone running and then shouting.

"Hey, my main guinea! Stump, how are ya? Ya comin' back?"

Vinnie saw Dwayne, a fellow basketball player, coming toward him. He had often thought about Dwayne and was glad to see him; and Dwayne was glad to see him. Dwayne came over and pushed down on Vinnie's head. He was about six feet, four inches. Vinnie was a mere five foot four. Charlie Ray called them Mutt and Jeff, but on the court, they were a winning pair.

"Hey, you got shorter," said Dwayne, laughing.

"Well, you sure as hell didn't. You're gonna be illegal soon," returned Vinnie, looking up at the smiling black face, and remembering how he used to kid Dwayne that the light off his teeth could blind an opponent.

Vinnie assured Dwayne that he was going to play this year, then went into the office to work on his class schedule. There didn't seem to be any problem, and Mr. Ray was able to get him into the courses he wanted, including the special programs at Harvard.

The morning classes went uneventfully. Vinnie found there would be more homework than he might want, but otherwise, no problems. A few students welcomed him back, but he was pretty much on his own.

At lunch, he was keeping to himself when he was jolted from his thoughts by someone sitting beside him and nudging him. Vinnie turned and saw Lucy, one of the black cheerleaders.

"Hey, Lucy, how are ya, how's the squad?"

"Good, we're in tryouts now. Some good kids coming up, and hopefully I'll be back cheering by February."

"Huh?" grunted Vinnie. "Why aren't you cheering 'til then?"

Lucy looked at him as if to say, Come on, dummy, open your eyes.

Vinnie sat up straight and looked at her quizzically. Then he noticed. Lucy was pregnant, very pregnant.

"Oh, I get it," said Vinnie, somewhat embarrassed. "You're gonna come back after it's born, aren't you?"

"Yeah, right away. Mr. Ray's gonna try to work something out with a day-care place. This ain't exactly my style, you know."

"Yeah," said Vinnie, turning back to his lunch. He didn't know quite what else to say.

"Well, it's good to have you back, Vin," said Lucy, standing up to leave.

"Yeah, thanks, it's good to be back," he smiled, "with friends." Lucy returned his smile and walked away.

Vinnie watched her. It seemed strange to see Lucy pregnant. She was young, only a junior, but it was not unusual for a girl to be pregnant at Roxbury High. At any one time, there might be six or eight pregnant girls in the school. They rarely got married.

Vinnie had once asked Mr. Ray why it seemed there were more pregnant girls here than, say, in Charlestown. He had been told there were a number of reasons. Education in birth control was scarce in the black community. There wasn't the stigma attached to unmarried pregnancy in the black community that there was in the white community, so it was easier for a girl to stay in school. There often wasn't enough money in the family for an abortion. And since there wasn't great pressure to get married, many girls saw no reason why they shouldn't continue to go to school.

A big plus in that line, Vinnie knew, was that Mr. Ray and the teachers always encouraged the girls to stay in school until the last possible moment. Vinnie had once heard Mr. Ray tell one girl it was better for her to be here than at home or looking for a bad job. And after the baby was born, it was the same story. "Come back to school; we'll work your schedule to account for the baby." Most of them did stay in school and went on to graduate. Vinnie often wondered what happened after that.

One thing he knew for sure was that it didn't happen this way in Charlestown. A pregnant girl in Charlestown High would be the center of attention, if she was stupid enough to stay in school. And she probably wouldn't be encouraged to stay in school. Her parents would be ashamed, and the neighbors would never let the family forget it for a moment. In a strong Catholic community, you just didn't get pregnant before you were married. Pregnant girls in Charlestown didn't stay in school; they often went to live with a relative out of town, or they very quickly got married.

The bell rang and Vinnie picked up his books and headed toward his next class. Suddenly a rush of uncertainty came over him. Over the summer, he had forgotten what it was like to be one of a handful of white students in a school full of blacks. He could feel the black students who didn't know him from last year look at him curiously.

He spotted another white student ahead of him in the hallway and, without thinking about it, hurried to catch up.

When Vinnie tapped him on the shoulder the boy turned suddenly, startled.

"You goin' to school here?" the boy asked.

"Yeah, sure. Vinnie Macioce."

"Lew Marten." They shook hands somewhat formally.

"Listen" — Lew pulled him to the side — "where are all the white kids, huh? This place is spooky."

"No, it's not. Honest. There are other white kids here. And all the Asian kids."

"Man, I had no idea." Lew shook his head. "We just moved here, and I thought there'd be more white kids. I don't think I'm gonna stick around. There's gotta be another school I can go to. You take your life in your hands comin' through the streets. What about you?"

"I went here last year. Had a chance to go someplace else this year, but wanted back here." Vinnie watched Lew's eyes open wide as he digested Vinnie's words.

"You did?" Lew asked incredulously.

"Yeah, it's a good school. You get used to being a minority. Just bothers you the first couple days. Most of the black kids are pretty nice to you. And the principal is a super guy. Everyone knows it."

Lew just stood there, bewildered. "What kind of trouble was there last year? Come on." He was getting impatient with Vinnie.

"Nothing special," replied Vinnie quickly. "Hey, you're lettin' first impressions get to you."

"I've heard some kids have been mugged around the neighborhood."

"Yeah, that's true."

Lew shook his head again. "Think more white kids will start comin'?"

Vinnie knew he had to be realistic.

"The problem is most of 'em won't even give it a chance. You should, though." He really wanted to persuade Lew. "The classes are good, the sports good, all types of special programs. Go some other place and you'll be lost in the shuffle."

"They sure can't lose sight of me here." Lew looked around at the stream of black faces.

"So what do you think?"

"Naw, just makes me feel real uncomfortable. I don't mind blacks, but I mind being the only white guy in the class. And the neighborhood really shits. Nope, this is my first day and my last day."

Vinnie stood in the corridor and watched Lew walk down the hall.

"Whatsa matta? Can't get along with the white kids, chump?" It was Wu.

"No, it's not that." He shook his head. "This joint never is gonna be really integrated is it?"

"You got it."

"No matter what it's like."

"You got it."

They started down the hall together. "That's a damn shame."

Epilogue

JULIE GRADUATED from South Boston High with a nursing scholarship to a local college. On her right hand, she proudly displays a South Boston High class ring and often shakes her head at how strange it looks against her black skin. Her two younger sisters now attend a much more peaceful South Boston High.

Laurie did not return to South Boston High until the next September. She graduated and now works as a sales clerk at the domestic counter of a small department store. She is engaged and hopes to be married as soon as her boyfriend gets out of the navy. They are already saving for a down payment on a small house three blocks from South Boston High.

Greg dropped out of Southie that spring. He bagged groceries for awhile, then pumped gas, and now drives a cab. He still talks about going back to night school, someday.

Officer McMaster is still riding a motorcycle. He hopes for promotions, but so far none have come his way. As the war over desegregation calmed, so did the one between Southie and himself. He and his wife still take the children to Southie every Sunday to visit.

Kevin made it through the school year and made two good friends along the way — one white, one black. He finished the King and is now a senior at Dorchester High in the vocational program. His family still lives in the small house on Dana Street, anxious as ever about their future.

Jerome never went back to school and never joined the Marines. He and his friends continued to hang around the project. Several of them, Jerome included, were recently convicted of car theft and assault and battery. Jerome received a one-year suspended sentence.

Tony now runs back kickoffs for a small college in Virginia. His scholarship pays for tuition and books, and he works in a local pizza joint to make up the rest. His mother, two brothers, and baby sister still live in the project. His mother is already planning a big graduation party for him. Jack now attends an Ivy League college. Annie is studying at a school of art in Boston.

Kim is a senior at Boston Technical High, one of three schools in the city that won't accept students unless they pass an entrance exam. She transferred out of Charlestown because it didn't offer the programs she wanted. Kim will start her training as a medical technician in June.

Linda's basement classroom finally grew into Hyde Park Academy. The academy, with about two hundred fifty students, was certified by the school committee, making it a legal institution. However, the college Linda hoped to attend would not accept all her credits so she was forced to attend public night school. She dropped out, though, and now works as a junior clerk at Boston City Hall. Her father is now active in a group monitoring morality in the media.

Vinnie graduated from Roxbury High. He took Jeanne Wu to the senior prom and supplied a case of champagne for the whole class. He now attends Harvard College on scholarship, and regularly returns to Roxbury High to visit Charlie Ray. Roxbury High, meanwhile, is fighting to stay off the list of schools being shut down in Boston because of declining enrollments.

Helen still works at Faulkner Hospital. She never could identify any of her assailants, and no charges were brought against anyone. She says she is bitter about the experience, but considers it an isolated case.

Christopher graduated from Quincy High and now attends the University of Massachusetts. His father, still bitter about busing, now pays higher taxes than ever.

Although he was accepted at several colleges, Larry opted to travel around the country for a year before going to college. The decision was made over his mother's strong protests, but with his father's blessings. Jesse had to stay a full extra year at Latin, but graduated near the middle of his class. Latin set up special tutorial programs for all black students who were behind. Jesse had his pick of several colleges, and now attends a state university on scholarship.

The Lee School still has not lost a kid. The first graders say they love it.

Time Line

1787. Petition to open Boston Public School System to black children is denied.

1854. Massachusetts State Legislature passes law abolishing public school segregation.

1965, April. Black parents protest at state capitol asking for an end to de facto segregation in the public schools and for better teachers, supplies, and facilities for their children.

1965, August. Massachusetts Racial Imbalance Act passed prohibiting public schools to be majority white or majority black.

1970, October. Census reveals 63 Boston schools are in violation of the 1965 Racial Imbalance Act.

1971, September. Boston School Committee reneges on promise to open the Lee School as an integrated school. State Board of Education votes to withhold state funds from Boston. City of Boston sues, state countersues.

1971, November. U.S. Department of Health, Education, and Welfare, finding that Boston operates a dual school system — one for blacks, one for whites — threatens to cut off federal funds.

1972, March. National Association for the Advancement of Colored People files class-action suit against the City of Boston on behalf of black students in the public schools.

1974, June 21. Federal Judge W. Arthur Garrity, Jr., rules that the City of Boston has been intentionally creating and perpetuating a segregated school system. Orders immediate desegregation to provide equal educational opportunity to all students.

1974, September. ROAR (Restore Our Unalienated Rights) is unveiled as national anti-busing organization. Louise Day Hicks is leader and founder.

1974, September 12. Boston Public Schools open under first desegregation plan. Buses from South Boston carrying black students are stoned.

1974, October 7. Black man is dragged from his car in South Boston and beaten by whites. Violence breaks out throughout the city, in both white and black communities.

1974, October 9. President Gerald Ford puts the 101st Airborne Division on "increased readiness" for possible assignment to the City of Boston to control violence.

1974, October 15. White student is stabbed at Hyde Park High School. Governor puts the national guard on alert.

1974, November. School boycotts called by anti-busing leaders. White students boycott sporadically throughout entire month.

1974, December 11. White student stabbed at South Boston High School. Schools in both South Boston and Roxbury are closed.

1974, December 16. Majority of Boston School Committee refuses to comply with court order requiring submission of complete desegregation plan.

1974, December 19. U.S. Federal Court of Appeals unanimously upholds Judge Garrity's desegregation ruling.

1975, March 19. ROAR rallies in Washington, D.C.

1975, May 10. Phase II of Boston desegregation plan, including colleges and businesses, is handed down by the federal court after the city fails to come up with its own plan.

1975, September 7. ROAR holds anti-busing rally in Boston.

1975, September 10. Boston schools open under the most massive show of police force in the history of any public school opening. Sporadic violence.

1975, September 11. Students begin regular marches out of Charlestown High School.

1975, December 9. The Boston School Committee loses control of South Boston High School. The school is placed under receivership, being run by the federal court.

1976, April 5. White students protesting busing on City Hall Plaza attack a black passerby with the staff of an American flag. Violence again spreads throughout the city.

1976, April 19. A white motorist is attacked by black youths as he is driving through a black neighborhood. Attack causes severe brain damage, and two years later, death.

1976, April 23. A Procession Against Violence is held through the streets of Boston. Fifty thousand people participate.

1976, September. Boston schools open peacefully. City calms down. Very few racial disturbances through the year. No major confrontations. Police presence exists only at a few high schools.

1977, 1978. These two school years see only a few racial disturbances within the schools. For the most part, desegregation seems behind the city.

1979, September. Buses carrying black students from South Boston High are stoned by white youths.

1979, September 28. A black football player, standing in the end zone with teammates at the Charlestown High School football field, is shot in the head. Police termed the shooting "a random racial shooting" by someone who just fired into a group of black football players.

1979, October 1. Pope John Paul II visits Boston and speaks on the subject of love and brotherhood.